James Hunter Crawford

Wild flowers of Scotland

James Hunter Crawford

Wild flowers of Scotland

ISBN/EAN: 9783743341852

Manufactured in Europe, USA, Canada, Australia, Japa

Cover: Foto ©ninafisch / pixelio.de

Manufactured and distributed by brebook publishing software (www.brebook.com)

James Hunter Crawford

Wild flowers of Scotland

Wild Flowers of Scotland

By J. H. CRAWFORD, F.L.S.

AUTHOR OF "WILD LIFE OF SCOTLAND," ETC.

ILLUSTRATIONS BY JOHN WILLIAMSON

LONDON: JOHN MACQUEEN

MDCCCXCVII

CONTENTS

INTRODUCTION

L ESS has been said in a pleasant way about
     the wild flowers than about the wild
animals of Scotland.

Yet our four-footed creatures are few, and their
tale easily told. Our wild birds, too, have been
sadly thinned out, with the exception of sea forms;
and these belong to other coasts as well. Birds
have wings, and can cross water.

Whereas the many wild flowers are well-nigh
untouched. Nor do they fly about from place to
place, but remain pretty much where they have been
all along. They are ours, in a sense in which
other living things are not.

Moreover, they are out of fellowship with the
wild flowers of other lands. There is no common
border across which they mingle with kindred

forms. Like ourselves, they have a semi-island character, and have grown into what they are by long ages spent within the Channel. They have been shaped and coloured here.

If the quest is not exciting, it is not therefore less interesting. Some of the ruder elements of sport are absent. We do not shoot them, nor do we hunt them with dogs.

Nevertheless, it is not all dainty basket-work in shaded woodland glade, or on sunny bank, seeing that Scotland is not made up of such mild features as these. To the venturesome there is abundant opportunity of showing what is in him.

If the ledge of coast-cliff, where the peregrine builds, is bad to get at, either from the grassy top, or from the bottom where the water gurgles, the crack in which the rare seaside flower roots itself is still more puzzling. It needs a cool head as well as a rope and a belt.

If only a bold man dare take the golden eagle's eggs from the face of a Grampian precipice, it needs a bolder one still to rob that little colony of alpines, faintly glowing, through the field-glass, five hundred feet above or below.

It thus appears that in a land like this the pursuit of the rarer wild flowers need not be lacking in manliness. If they do not run away, it is because they are safe from all but the boldest, who will blench at nothing, in some giddy place which no blue hare could reach, and where no mountain bird could perch.

Where wild animals thin out towards the tops of mountains until, it may be, only two are left, wild plants climb on ahead, scaling everything by the way, so that one who would follow them must be at least as hardy as a ptarmigan shooter. No scene so rude as to deter them, or so lofty as to keep them back. If they are not higher, it is because there is no greater height to reach.

They are in all sorts of cunning places, where a false step or too long a reach might be awkward. They hide in the shadow of the boulder, or peep from the crevice of the rock to see who may be the strange visitor, in solitudes so seldom disturbed by human footstep.

And the results at the close of a long day, when one has dropped down the mountain-side and perhaps got into his slippers, are certainly not less a matter of boast than the bag of game. One has at least the satisfaction of feeling that he has been among genuine wildlings, that have been left in those out - of - the - way places to fight their own battle with natural enemies.

I have followed both plant and animal, with no view of taking either egg or flower out of its picturesque or wild setting, and I owe more of my delight in wild nature and my knowledge of Scotland to the former than to the latter.

.   .   .   .   .   .

The quest for flowers has led me by the seaside, within the spray of the breakers; inland—over spring meadows passionate with blossoming, through brakes glowing with broom, along lanes scented with the May; upland, beyond the purple and pink heather zones, to where the mountain breezes play most freely.

My wish is to take those who care to follow, by the same pleasant ways, to the same goal. I shall begin low down, and among familiar things, only so far Scots, that in some cases they have had to harden themselves to our soil and climate.

" You are not going to give us everything found here ? " said one.

"Oh dear, no! Nothing is further from my thoughts."

A few typical forms in a natural setting, livened by some incident or course of events in which I shared, or stood by to witness; and that is all.

Among others, the wild flowers of these benty sea-coast stretches, known in their natural state as links; and that for a certain reason, which I shall proceed to give.

No pleasanter way can there be of spending the hot hours of a summer day than on some royal mantle of purple thyme, or some humbler couch of yellow bed-straw, looking away over the lit and shaded grasses; and, yielding to the drowsy influence, to tilt the cap over the face, and to go to sleep to the whispering of the sea within the shell of the ear.

Of seaside thyme, or humbler bed-straw, there will soon be none. As these scenes are being invaded and re-turfed, this sketch may come to be interesting as a picture of what used to be.

In St. Andrews—that Mecca of golf—until the other day, a margin of natural bents was left between the new course and the sea. Visitors will recall the bright picture on the sunny afternoons of their stay, filled in by attractive groups, of which they may have formed one.

Even this strip has been taken away. And a whisper is passing round that the lack of walking-room may be supplied by wounding the sides of perhaps the most picturesque sand-dunes in the country. This would be worse even than driving away the links flowers, and denying an afternoon · siesta in the hot sun to all who are not prepared for a rude awakening.

From the seaside and the plain, where so much is common, I shall enter the fastnesses in search of what is peculiarly Scots, and wade through the belt of shrubs to the alpine region beyond.

From the mountain-top, as a coign of vantage, I shall gaze away north, over the milder Shetlands, to where mountain forms with us grow at sea-level, and are known no longer as alpines, but as arctics.

From Nansen's *Farthest North* I borrow a nearer view of these arctic lowlands.

"In the evening we at last reached the islands, and for the first time for two years had bare land under foot. The delight was indescribable, and was not lessened when, in a little sheltered corner among the stones, we found beautiful poppies and snowy saxifrages."

WILD FLOWERS OF SCOTLAND

I

THE FLOWERS OF SPRING

THE daisy never dies. The eye of the winter as of the summer day, it is *bellis perennis*, in a double sense: a thing of beauty, throughout the year, and throughout the years.

So early do some plants flower, that they seem to belong as much to the past as to the coming season. Among such is the furze or whin. On any open winter day it may be traced, by its cocoanut scent, to where it lights up the leeside of turf dyke, or wood strip with its dark yellow blossoms. But for the bareness of the willow, which has not yet hung out a single catkin, the stillness of the woods, broken only by the drowsy

2

noises of the gold-crests in the fir-trees, and the midday shadows falling down the coloured sunlight of the fallow field, one might be lulled, for a time, into forgetfulness of the season.

With little shelter except the sand-dunes, the whin is known to flower as early as November. Thenceforward it continues to make the desolate places of the land rejoice, until the golfers come out on the links, and the linties begin to build inside.

Daisy and whin have no other message than the mildness of the air: it may be before or after Christmas. Neither takes any part in Nature's calendar, so that one can tell what time of year it is.

The earliest flower with a definite beginning, whose appearance one knows when to look for, is the colt's-foot. It is not much of a flower in appearance: not unlike a rather indifferent dandelion, and of the same order. It is also a plant of somewhat evil omen, showing poverty or neglect. But it is without a rival when, with its ·bright rays and disc of still warmer hue, it touches up the faded grasses; and where there is no choice, one is not disposed to be critical.

The spring note of the missel-thrush would

miss its welcome if it came a little later, when
the air was already thrilling with richer melodies.
By the way, the singing came before the budding.
The birds, and not the flowers, are the true heralds
of spring. Ere the date of the colt's-foot, say in
early March, the mavis has eclipsed his bigger
cousin, and the blackbird has trolled out his first
mellow note. Nevertheless, this somewhat squalid
forerunner of the flowers, like the earliest of the
birds, has a welcome all to itself.

The colt's-foot is yellow. The first crocus to
touch the dark soil of the garden is yellow. The
beauty with which the daffodil takes the winds of
March is yellow. Whatever plant has more hues
than one, likes to show the yellow first.

Yellow is said to be the primitive colour: that
which broke out over the prevailing green of the
ancient earth, and began the long and increas-
ingly close fellowship between bright insect and
bright plant.

Spring is an early season. Before those who
have eyes to see, each year repeats the story of the
earth. Yellow is the complexion of spring, steal-
ing over the prevailing green of our moist winters.
The languid bee crawls from straw hive or hole
in the turf dyke, and, shaking out his cramped

wings, makes, with uncertain aim, begotten of lessened use and vitality, for the yellow spot.

The lesser celandine is also yellow when it is young and fresh, though it soon bleaches into white. Its star-like appearance is borrowed from the many-pointed rays — eight, or nine. This feature marks it out among the flowers, were there any so soon besides the colt's-foot to confuse it with—gives it, so to speak, a certain individuality.

By the high roads, which, happily at the time, are not quite so dusty as they afterward become, it grows in a stunted form, and wears an away-from-home look.

It belongs to the burn-sides, where it brightens the broken passage of the angler from current to current and from pool to pool. Its associations are with running water and early trouting. Only those who have seen the dark green leaves against the reddish brown bank, and the yellow star against the dark green leaves, or both leaf and star standing out against the neutral-tinted stream, can tell all the celandine is. Only those, too, who know it as one of many pleasant impressions.

Nor is it the only flower which one has learned to like, less for itself than because of scene and

21

surrounding. One who has been abroad, rod in hand, can never afterward separate the spring celandine from the flushed stream, such as we have at that season, the long shadows, the pink and black spots of the newly-landed trout, and all the fresh emotions attending the first cast and catch after a winter's fast.

It is known as Wordsworth's flower. Had he been an enthusiastic angler we could have understood the choice, because, for reasons just stated, all the members of the fraternity are disposed to appraise it beyond its merits. But being only an unattached admirer in search of beauty, the preference is more puzzling. He expressed his admiration in a sonnet which I would rather not quote. The Ayrshire poet moralised over the daisy, and Tennyson had the taste to follow so good an example. The Westmoreland poet must needs moralise over something else. I question whether the reputation, either of flower or poet, is very much bettered thereby.

The place of the fading celandine is filled by the anemone. Beginning with a pink bud, it opens into a white flower. It has a tendency to grow in patches, netted by underground stolons. The delicately cut foliage is in itself a delight. It is

called nemorosa because it is found in woods, and
anemone because it is found in windy places.
Thus we get the singular combination "anemone
nemorosa," which seems rather a contradiction in
terms.   The wood is still.   The woodland storm
no more troubles the sheltered glades where the
anemones dwell, than the lash of waves reaches
the depths of ocean.   Far overhead the wind
bends the topmost branches, and sings a spiritual-
ised version of the ruder song of the sea.   Those
who find it growing in the wilds may call it
anemone, and those who come upon the self-same
plant in the woods may call it nemorosa; and both
will then be satisfied.

The wood anemone creeps up the hillsides.   On
that playground of theirs the breezes deal gently
with their favourite, fanning it into healthy
motion, without scattering its loose flower.   There
it may chance to meet a sister.

The blue mountain anemone takes wood or open
with equal thanks.   No other anemones grow wild
in Scotland.   The summer pasque flower keeps to
the chalk downs, of which we have none.

At much the same time, in much the same places
as the anemone, appears the primrose; at least it
shares the shadier half of the wind flower's domain.

More impatient of the wind, it may be called a
shade flower. It loves the woods where the sunshine is broken into patches, and finds out all sorts
of sheltered corners, or primrose niches. Sometimes it gets its roots into a crack of the rock
overlooking a woodland pool, in which it can see
itself.

It is by no means the first rose, as its name
would seem to imply; nor is it a rose at all, any
more than a jelly-fish is a fish. The only explanation I can offer of this second double name is that,
whereas the earlier forms grow in out-of-the-way
places, are scentless, and appear when out-of-door
life has scarce as yet begun, the primrose is by
the brookside, where the girls play; in the strip
of wood, where the boys go a-nesting; and all
on those bright days when the sun has taken the
chill off the air and sufficiently dried the natural
playgrounds.

Well do I remember finding my first thrush's
nest, under the green rosette with its crown of
yellow. The spotted breast of the sitter, the
spotted blue eggs when she arose, the crossing
shadows, and the prattle of the burn, form a
picture which has not yet perceptibly faded.

This fixes the date of the flower, according to

my favourite way of reckoning, at the nesting-
time of the song thrush; or, to descend to plain
prose, somewhere between March and May. Impatient thrushes build, and early primroses blow,
sooner; and I have found both eggs and flowers
later. But the nesting and the blossoming reach
their height together; so that on the day one
gathers the largest handful of flowers, he will
startle most sitting birds among the bushes.

This is the first flower to attract attention: the
first scented flower; and as every flower is a rose
to the vulgar, so this is the primrose.

The primulas—of which our primrose is one—
range from the deepest dells to the highest
mountains. Strangely enough, none of the strictly
mountain primulas appear in Scotland, the home
of British alpines. Our colour is yellow—in the
primrose of a very pale cast, indefinitely sweet,
like the scent of the flower; deepening in hue
in the cowslip. According to their wont, the
yellows come in spring.

We have two lilacs later in the season. One
is in the north, and the other in the south. Both
are very local. So very slight is the hold of the
southern species that it can scarcely be regarded
as Scots. The other we shall meet again. Both

are moorland, or sub-alpine. Lilac and purple are
the mountain colours. Happy is the man who,
in garden, rockery, or greenhouse, gathers the
primulas of Europe round those of Scotland.

Commonest of a lovely family, the dog violet
shares the windy and exposed half of the anemone's
domain. I like to think of it on the bank, sloping
down to ditch or stream, with the nest of the
yellow-hammer hard by. There it so overtops the
short, fresh grass, that every tiny speck of blue is
seen. Hand in hand, like sisters born, it climbs
the slope with the anemone, and goes just about
as high.

It passes under the shadow far enough to join
the primroses. There it grows larger, if more
faintly hued flowers; and changes its name to the
wood violet. The smaller, deeper blue bank violet
is better. Whereas the shade-loving primrose
sometimes wanders out into the open, the violet of
the open enters the shades. Together with the
anemone, primrose and violet make fairy glades
worth searching out.

The three-coloured violet gets the credit of being
parent to our garden pansies. A little later than
the first appearance of the dog violets,—for it will
save space elsewhere if I chat about some of the

summer friends of these spring flowers,—heartsease
scatters over the drier turf.   On climbing the
dykes into the grain field, it grows a long stem, at
the expense of the blossom.   There is some reason
to suppose that the climbing has been the other
way.   Introduced with the grain, it may have
crossed to the meadows, where it shortened its
stalk, to the benefit of the flower.

Does heartsease climb the mountains, away
beyond the utmost limit of the dog violet ?   Does
it there drop white and blue—all its shades save
one—and become the yellow mountain violet ?
If I am justified in linking the three-hued violet
of the plain with the one-hued mountain violet,
across the gap between where neither grows, then
the heartsease may be a native after all : may have
come down the slopes, and not over the dyke.   The
ascent, if such there was, must be pretty far back.

Still another violet haunts the marshes: not
simply wet places, but genuine old bogs, which
have never been reclaimed, and whose date must
be primeval.

It recalls ankle-deep wading through mossy
and peaty stretches, with frequent quickening of
the motion, and jumps, lest the sinking should be
inconveniently deep.

Never shall I forget one sunrise two thousand feet among the Perthshire hills, in a haunt of the marsh violet—the soaking mosses, the deep black pools which no summer heat could dry up; nor the plight I was in; nor the comments passed when, toward six in the morning, I appeared at my lodging by the Ardle side.

Blue in colour like the dog violet, it differs mainly in the roundness of the leaf—rounder even than that of the sweet violet.

A fancy sometimes helps one. I have never been able to disassociate the violets, so strangely perfect among the native wild flowers, from the tits, so strangely perfect among the native wild birds. Blue is the predominant colour in both; the number of species is the same; and the moist stretches which yield the marsh violet yield also the marsh tit.

Still in wet places, though not so old, nor wild, nor far away, appear two other moisture lovers, familiar to those who never heard of the marsh violet, and chiefly to all readers of *The May Queen*.

By the meadow trenches blow the faint sweet cuckoo flowers,
And the wild marsh marigold shines like fire in swamps
and hollows grey.

Permanent pasture is not common in Scotland. Few dry meadows lighten at spring-time with the passionate blossoming of those in the South. Our green stretches are mainly the overflow of streams —marshes rather than meadows.

Raw enough at other times, and in winter often impassable, such scenes become charming when, in April, a bright sisterhood of flowers is let loose over them. Here and there, among the pinks are glowing yellows.

Then the spring buttercups come out among the daisies of the bank, yielding the most charming effects with the simplest touches. The first is that with the bulb at the roots, to make it independent of the niggardness of the season; and the pale sepals, bent back so quaintly against the stem.

The later fibrous-rooted buttercups follow; the taller of them to o'ertop the lengthening grasses, and glisten among the brown panicles with a second effect, not less simple or charming than that among the daisies.

While this lasts, Spring is abroad as if she had taken lovely shape, visibly scattering from her lap; and he who would find her will do well to go to such grassy banks, and look there. If the beauty is not passionate, it is altogether satisfying.

II

THE BLUE BELLS

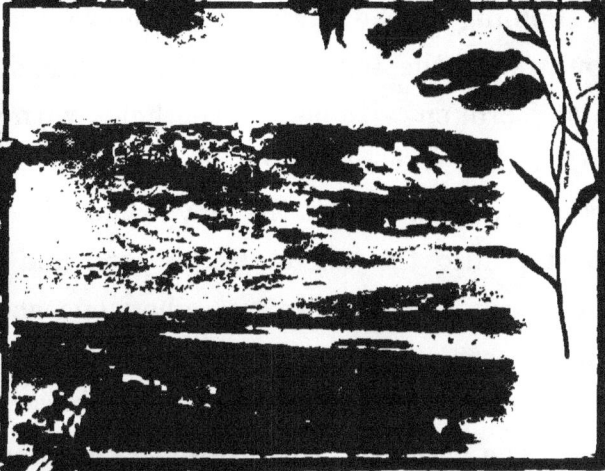

A FORTNIGHT after I have gathered the last handful of perfect flowers from the fading anemones, and looked on the primroses at their best, I return to the woods.

A blue mist steals over the bank running down to the stream. There is a sheen through the undergrowth, as of beauty in hiding.

It is an April day, somewhat past the middle of the month, between the leafing of the sloe and the blossoming of the hawthorn. The walk across the country by the bursting hedgerows was delightful. A sky broken with clouds, the fields with shadows, and a sun warm enough to make the shelter of trees grateful. Just the day when one has only to step into the shade to be cool, and out into the sunshine to be warm: when one cheek is in the pleasant sunshine, and the other in the cool shadow.

On the way, the birds were alert and busy. The gush of song on either hand was incessant, ever breaking out afresh and ahead, as if I were passing along a lane bordered on either side by melody; or, rather, through an arch, of which the lark's song was the highest part. Flashes of fresh colour appeared for a moment, as the greenfinch passed from tree to tree, and the yellow-hammer from hedge to hedge. Beauty as well as melody bordered and arched the lanes. One cannot mistake the presence of spring in April.

The dry slope of woodland bank is inviting.

One can drink in the exceeding loveliness of such surroundings better when he is lying down. The shadows over the current, and up the far bank fall so pleasantly across the spirit. Only in so far as there are spirit shadows can we see their beauty. No tracery in Nature is more delicate than that above, except that shadow tracery of twigs and bursting buds below. One can scarce help being beautiful in soul while he lies here. He is only reflecting.

The chaffinch, without whose spring note the budding woods would scarcely seem themselves, is now in full song. If the lay is not sweet, it is woodland, which is far better, and shows how much music owes to the scene in which we delight to hear it. No other song would please so much.

The scent as well as the complexion of the den has changed. It is no longer the spiritual essence— so faintly sweet when diffused through the outer air—of primrose. At least not altogether; though there, it is hard to detect. Something heavier— too heavy in the concentrated sweetness into which it is gathered in the close defile between the banks —overpowers the rest.

The primroses are still abroad among the wood grasses, or beside the mossy stump, or under the bole of the fallen tree. Scattered here and there, according to their wont, they charm the eye that wanders over the woodland floor, with their picturesque setting and frequent surprises. No two are placed exactly alike.

The habit of the hyacinth is different. With less genius for setting, it becomes picturesque only when seen at a distance. More prodigal of its favours, it spreads out in sheets, broken only by the tree boles under the lights and shadows. Within its areas, nor blade nor leaf of aught else is suffered to appear. I am crushing scores of them where I lie; and I am lying here simply because I could find no other place where they were not.

All round about me, within easy reach of my hand, the pendent blossoms hang down the stalks, so that I can see all I want without pulling or breaking. When I lay my head back, a flower ripples over either cheek in hyacinthine locks of blue.

That it belongs to the lilies is made plain even by the grass-like leaves. And, like the rest of that lovely family, it is able, by a certain natural providence, to make an early start. I cut a little square in the turf round the stem, and dig the whole plant out. And there, half a foot down in the brown mould, is the store of food laid up in the past season against the spring.

Several flowers are so closely woven-in with the name of our country, that we, who were born here, can scarcely recall the day we thought of them apart. When we begin "the blue bells," we feel as if we had not said enough till we add "of Scotland."

The blue bell has found its way into song, as blooming more distinctly than any other wild flower in the author's mental picture of the land. Others have had some favourite object chosen from amid the scenes where they were reared, some symbol of so much combined love of nature and patriotism as they possessed. An exile passionately recalled Scotland by "the broom that hung its tassels on the lea," and, among birds, by the "lintie's sang." Being destitute of imagination or the power of expression, we borrow from the more gifted. And it is amusing how fervently some of us, when in poetic vein, sing of what we never saw, and exult in what we never cared for.

In the esteem of this man, the blue bell is not only worthy of Scotland, but also more to be proud of than the "jasmine bowers and rose-covered

3

dells " of sunnier lands. And we echo the sentiment, without being quite sure what is meant.

There happen to be two bells, or rather bell-like
flowers, each of which might well advance its
claims. And the unstinted praise may well lead to
a battle or duel of the flowers. The earlier in the
field is the wild hyacinth.

I bend one of the stalks gently toward me.
The petals close, and turn out at the tip into a
delicate vase shape. It is a Scots bell, although
not distinctively so. And there is no valid reason
to be found in the beauty of the plant, in the
charm it lends to hundreds of our dells, in the
character it gives to our spring woodlands, in the
delight it yields to all lovers of nature, and in the
gap it would leave if it deserted its haunts—for
what else would fill up the space which divides the
primrose and the summer flowers ?—why it should
not be the Scottish Blue Bell.

True, it is not found everywhere. Many country-
sides are without it. Many shady places may be
searched without the tell-tale odour revealing its
presence, and guiding to its twilight domain.
Many dells as promising as this have to supply the
want as best they can.

But wherever it is, it can scarcely escape the

attention of the least observant, or fail to awaken
the enthusiasm of the least impressionable. Every
schoolboy on the Saturday half-holiday visits its
haunts for the nests of the rarest birds, and gathers
handfuls to scatter on the way home. Every
country maiden from the surrounding cotter
houses pushes it among her locks.

"My little girl with the golden hair and the soft
eyes, what do you like?" "To be among the wood
hyacinths."

Beyond the margin of the wood, the hyacinths
flow over the bank among the brambles and trailing roses. The white-throat and rose linnet weave
their nests among the scented twigs; and the
yellow-hammer builds among the grasses, where
the long pleasant days of sitting may be shaded by
the bells.

A fortnight or so after the blue hyacinths have
faded,—say about the end of June, when already
every egg has been chipped, and the birds are busy
feeding their second brood amid the thickening
undergrowth,—a second flower of Scotland makes
its appearance.

It is no longer vase-shaped, but bell-shaped;
indeed, it is one of the true bells, with all its petals
joined into one. If there is anything lovelier than

a lily, it is a campanula, which is just another name for bell.   And this is the most delicate of the graceful family to which it belongs.

Here everything is etherealised, only sufficient substance being used to indicate and preserve the form.   If it were not prejudging the case, one might be disposed to pronounce it the most perfect in shape of all flowers, either wild or cultivated, in Scotland or elsewhere.

There is no stiffness about it, like the other ; no stout stem whereon to suspend heavy-textured blossoms.   If ever bell were tremblingly hung, this one is.   It vibrates to the slightest stirring of the air ; and when is the air still in its exposed haunts ?   It seeks the open wastes, as pleasanter for the breathless days than the sheltered wood-lands.

Not yet has it been decided how the name arose ; and the spelling is left very much to individual imagination and taste.   Where the choice is between two such names, equally poetic and suggestive, there is really no hurry.   The pity would be to lose either of them.

If it is hair bell, the reference is to the exquisite poising of the blossom on the hair-like stem.   If hare bell, still fresher associations with the moorland are conveyed. It must mean that the hare has its form where the flowers grow; and, on its passage to and fro, rings from the fairy bells—

> Their wandering chimes to vagrant butterflies.

The extreme delicacy lends not only grace, but safety as well. Whereas other moorland plants protect themselves from the unchecked storms, or the tread of animals, in various coarser ways, this has learned from nature the gentler art of conquering by knowing when to yield.

> E'en the slight hare bell raised its head
> Elastic from her airy tread.

Scott meant this as a compliment to the grace of Helen Douglas; but half of it belongs to the flower. Clumsier feet by far than those of the Lady of the Lake may tread, and the stem will spring back again uninjured. The bell, so fragile seeming, has simply sunk among the soft grass or moss, and will shake itself into perfect form again as soon as the pressure has passed, and it is lifted into air.

I have seen a limb torn from the tough birch, or a moorland pine uprooted, but I never saw a hare bell crushed—beyond the power of rising and shaking out its creases again—by anything lighter than a cart-wheel; and not always by that.

This bell has no scent. No second inducement is

needed to those vagrant butterflies. So far, it stands at a disadvantage with its rival. Growing singly or in clusters, and not in masses, it does not attract the eye from a distance, as a glow of colour. But it is almost everywhere, which the other is not. It fringes the edges of the cornfields, climbs the mountain-sides till it meets the lower alpines, where I have seen it white as the mountain hares of winter; and runs down to the coast till it is washed by the salt spray, where I have also seen it white: on either site, when bleached, it scarcely looks like itself.

Chiefly is it a moorland wildling, companion of the meadow pipit and the nesting plover. And in such moors Scotland abounds. From June onward, every golf-ball driven on St. Andrews links rings the wandering chimes to the blue seaside butterflies. Levelled for a moment, it swiftly rises again, and, ere the golfer passes, it is already trembling in the light breeze as if nothing had happened.

It is gathered by school children, in those delightful autumn weeks spent by the seaside or on inland moor. It blooms for a while along with the marguerite, to whose calm beauty it adds fairy-like grace. And when the reign of marguerite is over, it fills the vases of æsthetic maidens, adding to, and borrowing the delicacy of the lighter grasses which tremble beside it. Thus it has all the claims of its tenderer loveliness, of its wider-spread, and its closer sympathy with the genius of the land to be recalled, whenever Scotland is named.

But why worry oneself between two such fair claimants? Why not, with honest Cassio, confess each to be more excellent than the other? A queen may surely reign in Spain while another reigns in England, and the earth prove large enough for both. In like manner two fairy queens may reign at once, so long as one holds her court on the moor and the other in the woods. Why not pay devoirs to the hare bell in the open, and change our allegiance on passing beneath the branches. Two fairy queens can reign in different places at the same time, and all beauty is not gathered into one bell, any more than into one face.

But even this is not a full statement of the case. Both are not abroad on the earth, even in their different scenes, at the same time. Then what excuse is there for rivalry? Who wants a cessation in the reign of beauty, or even an interregnum?

Let us divide the kingdom between them, mak-

ing the hyacinth queen for life.   All the spring
we shall feel at liberty to pay court to her, lying
out among the trembling shadows, changing as the
buds open into leaves.   Until the shilfa's song
begins to lose its early freshness, and the warbler's
lay awakens, we shall make the rocky den echo to
our tuneful song, "The Blue Bells of Scotland."

And when at length the woods become faint
with heat: then on the breezy moor, or near "the
beached margent of the sea," where dance our
ringlets to the whistling wind, to the wandering
chimes of that other bell we shall finish our song,

"The Scottish Blue Bells."

III

THE GARDEN AND THE WILDS

THE garden is a natural nursery ; and the older it is, the larger its share in the wild flowers of the surrounding country-side is likely to be. Only by canopying the whole over and setting guards at the gate could escapes be prevented, and the line between native and cultivated kept sharp and distinct.

Seeds rise on the lightest breeze, and may be borne miles away before they come to rest. And if by field-side, or the margin of the wood they find conditions to suit them, they will spring. At the autumn thinning, clumps are thrown over the wall, which take root on the other side and spread away outward, surely if slowly.

Sometimes an æsthetic member of a family will plant a cutting of some favourite flower in one of her woodland or stream-side haunts. And, long after, the touch of a vanished hand is seen there by some curious passer-by.

It is not many years since gentle hands scattered English wildlings over a Scots park, and planted garden flowers in a Scots woodland.   And there they are now to witness if I lie.   I could take anyone to the scene and point them out.   By the somewhat sad fortune which banishes daughters from their homes when a property changes hands, the planters are no longer there to watch their coming   and   going,   as   they   did   for   many seasons.

And there they are likely to remain.   I thought at the time that greater care might have been taken in the choosing : that double flowers and those of strange hues might have been left out.

But nature will be sure to put that right by and by.   The plants will revert to the simpler state : will yield up all their petals save one outer rim ; will agree on some single hue, probably that they wore before their captivity : and so recover their lost likeness to their wild brethren.   And, in years to come, delighted wanderers over the grass, or within the shades, will wonder why this corner is so much richer than the rest of the scene of which it forms a part. ·

Frequently I come upon a curious patch of confusion, where a few cultivated plants are struggling and fairly well holding their own, amid a promiscuous crowd of such pushing plebeians as groundsel, chickweed, and purple dead nettle. A ridge, not more than a foot high, enclosing a space, is all that tells of the site of some peasant's cottage, pulled down, not too soon, probably, for the well-being of its inmates.

In one of my walks I saw a daffodil growing on the banks of a rill. The leaves were long and green, the flowers large, yellow, and single. The whole plant was so healthy and happy-looking that I thought I had never seen a daffodil before. Plainly it was better satisfied with its fresh surrounding, than if it had been in some dry and dusty enclosure. No wonder, seeing that it is naturally a lover of such moist places.

The scene was shut in from the world on every side by a tree-crested ridge. Few came by in a day. The nearest cottage was a long field's-breadth away. I looked for some trace of recent planting. The turf was firm, as though long undisturbed.

For miles around there was no wild daffodil besides. I question if the county, had it been

searched from end to end,—I had been over most
of it,—would have yielded such another clump.
In some strange way, the flower had got there.
The scene suggested an æsthetic origin.

Only yesterday I plucked a crimson sprig from
a wild American currant, to lighten up a little
natural bouquet of brown wood moss and green
hawthorn leaf. The bush was growing vigorously
and flowering freely in the middle of a wood, a
mile and a half from any town.

How far this element goes to swell the sum of
our wild flowers it were extremely difficult to say.
But it seems fairly certain that, were all the
escapes from gardens deducted, a less bulky
volume would contain the natives.

To those who have watched the process—who
have all but seen the flight of the seeds over the
garden wall; who have certainly been at the birth
of the strange seedlings, under the shadow of the
wood, or on the moist stream-side bank; who have
traced, season by season, the creeping of the
garden parings away from the wall—the possible
additions from this source will seem scarcely
capable of exaggeration. And, on each discovery,
they will turn over the pages of their handbook
with fresh interest and curiosity.

I have seen many such escapes, both swift-winged and slow-footed, that are likely to make good their hold and increase their distance from the source, until the connection is broken. I could run over many more that happened not so long ago. These are now as well able to look after themselves as their neighbours, and are securely sandwiched in print, between two of the oldest inhabitants.

The pace would be quickened, and many another surprise greet one by the way, but that a garden flower in the wilds is no sooner detected than uprooted, and transferred within some other enclosure. I have often marked the showy fugitive, and next time I came by have missed it. A check on the too rapid increase of quickly-spreading species is not altogether a disadvantage, and a second check on the less ready admission of aliens might be a further benefit. It seems a pity to confuse, so as almost to lose sight of, our native lowland flora.

But for this acquisitiveness there is no reason why "none - so - pretty," which is at once the commonest garden plant, and one of the three British alpines absent from Scotland, should not be familiar at the roadside. Almost invariably it marks the site of abandoned cottages, and blooms round the outside of old garden walls; and so far from being discontented, it seems rather glad to get back to a wild state again.

I find the neighbourhood of ancient fortresses often rich in their wild flowers.

Within the enclosure of Craigmillar Castle grows the French sorrel. Thence it seems to have spread into the south of Scotland and the north of England.

The date of its coming was the sixteenth century. The vanished hand, in this case, that of Mary Queen of Scots. Amid her amiable weaknesses, Mary seems to have included a liking for plants, and may almost be traced from place to place by the relics she has left behind. Archangelica appeared in 1568, a year or two after the return from France, and may with some probability also be credited to Mary.

A Forfarshire den which I am in the habit of visiting, is noted among dens for its depth of shade, and the wealth of the flowering and flowerless plants. There true wildlings grow along with many a suspicious native. Everyone knows that Solomon's seal is much more difficult to get rid of than to plant. On being carried or thrown out of the garden, it will run its stolons under the outside soil in quite a get-rid-of-me-if-you-can sort of way. At one time it must have been placed there with a view of enriching the flora of the den.

Now it chances that on the top of the rock, a hundred feet or more above, there stands a castle of more than ordinary interest, as contesting with another the honour of being "The bonnie house o' Airlie." The vanished hand may have stretched from there. We cannot now deny the plant a place

among our Scottish wild flowers, without including
many another of the same den in our *Index Ex-
purgatorius.*

A defile of much more modest dimensions seems
even richer than this, inasmuch as the many rarities
are gathered into a narrower space. It has been
called a paradise of flowers. I always suspect these
paradises, where the wildlings I had searched for,
separately, over many miles, are all huddled within
a few yards, and mingled with other flowers not
growing elsewhere outside an enclosure. I find
myself asking for a reason.

Early in the year the rocks dipping steeply down
to the cool water are covered over with the great
heart-shaped leaves, and brightened with the big
yellow flowers of Leopard's bane. A faint sweet
smell woos me aside to the violets growing among
the grasses of a bank. Though acquainted with
every yard of the country, I know no other bank
on which the sweet violet nods. Why should it be
here ?

Not fifty yards away, on the very edge of the
rocks o'ertopping the Leopard's bane, is another
castle of sixteenth-century date, once in possession
of the Grahams, kinsmen of "Bonnie Dundee."
Not much more than a stone's - throw away,

a quaint building marks the site of Claver-
house itself.

It may be that there were hands gentle enough
for the work even in that rude fortress, and that

these things may have been planted much
about the same time that Mary was enriching
the garden of Craigmillar Castle.   At all
events, this place was inhabited, and either

4

the gentle or the simple must have placed them there.

If one looks for rare things in the neighbourhood of castles, the rude engagements of whose inhabitants left them neither time nor taste for trifles, and whose women had often to unsex themselves; much more confidently may he turn to the peaceful surroundings of monasteries, and the placid lives of monks. So much is said against these persons, who, if the truth were kown, were probably neither better nor worse than modern divines, that it is pleasant to record something in their favour. And naturalists have reason to be grateful to them for more than one service.

On the north bank of the Tay, not far from the bridge, there are certain banks and woods widely known for the luxuriance of their flowers. The primroses are taller and more sweetly pale and scented than elsewhere, and, contrary to their habit, grow so close together, as to preserve through April and May an almost unbroken sheet of colour. The atmosphere is delightful.

Hither the Dundee maidens appear, to gather, not one by one, but in handfuls; and, furnished all too soon with what they come for, linger about until the evening, and return with baskets which freshen the streets and the jaded passers-by.

Above the pale and lowly primroses rise, upon their stalks, the darker-coloured cowslips. Now, the cowslip is not nearly so common in Scotland as in England; partly, perhaps, for the want of dry permanent pasture. Such cowslips, as we have, frequently find niches for themselves in the curious corners of woods.

Nor do the Scots cowslips look quite the same as those found growing on the English meadows. The smaller paler flowers of the latter give it a more truly wild look. Here the whole plant is larger, and more like the garden variety. This may be partly accounted for by its woodland haunts, where the struggle for existence is not so keen as in the meadow; or, when

growing in the open, may point to a more suspicious origin.

It might be too much to say that the cowslip is
not native to Scotland.   But, wherever it grows in
such abundance, in company with a profusion of
common flowers of the sweeter kinds, the hand of
man has probably had something to do with it.
And the only hands, vanished all of them, that could
have so enriched these Balmerino banks, and so
added to the charm of the scene and the happiness
of the lives to come after, belonged to the monks
of the adjacent monastery.

Where primroses and cowslips have grown so
long together in sweet fellowship, one may pretty
confidently start on the pleasant hunt for oxlips.
If Oberon knows a bank whereon the oxlip grows,
depend upon it, the cowslip is in the meadow, and
the primrose in the wood hard by.   This form is
easily picked out, even at a distance, by the larger
flower of the primrose on the common stalk of
the cowslip.

Hybrids between closely-related species, in plants
as well as animals, are doubtless commoner than
we are aware of.   All that is needful, in many
cases, is that the parent forms mingle freely on the
same scene.   But this is not always so easy to

detect, nor does it occur in the same marked degree. Violets, albeit approaching as closely as primrose and cowslip do, on the common margin of wood and meadow, modestly veil their attachment. If oxlips are not more frequently observed in Scotland, it is simply for the lack of cowslips.

A rarer and more undoubted legacy of these Balmerino monks is "the lily of the valley." Unhappily, it is an example also of the tendency of attractive plants, when they are sweet-scented as well, to disappear behind the garden wall. There is reason to believe that its tenure of Balmerino is already a thing of the past. The same fate must have attended it elsewhere. Like "none-so-pretty," it remains and thrives when the last stone of the cottage has fallen, and, by the aid of its underground stolons, spreads marvellously amid the rubbish.

It is so rare in Scotland, that many lovers of wild flowers who have searched the country well-nigh all over, never saw it growing wild. Here its presence suggests the vanished hand.

Guide-books tell us that, common in England, it thins out toward these boreal regions. As if it were the most natural thing in the world for a wild flower, at once so lovely and shelter-loving, to select the shade and rich depths of southern woodlands.

A closer acquaintance with its true nature shows the preference to be rather strange than otherwise. So far from being delicate, it is one of the hardiest of wild flowers; so far from being a shy woodland plant, it has no objection to stare the sun in the face.

The lily of the valley can, on occasion, become the lily of the mountain. Travellers to Norway find it growing in great abundance on bare rocks, near the perpetual snow-line.

Like many another, it may have come too late to the edge of the channel, and been debarred from crossing by the inflowing of the water. Afterward, it may have been introduced into English woods, mainly through the gardens; and much about the same time to the banks of the Tay. Nor are these the only gifts we owe to the monks; nor the rarest flowers that grow, or grew but yesterday, around the old monastery of Balmerino.

IV

WHIN AND BROOM

I N the later spring the country-side is touched
all over with colour—in lines, and patches, and
masses.

The lines mark out the rough margins of the
ploughed fields, just under the dividing fences,
or light up the edges of woods, or follow the
course of the burns. The patches crown the
knobs of hard rock rising above the general
level. The masses spread out over areas of
waste land, or along the lower slopes of the
hills.

Yellow, as yet, is the only wear; yellow in its
utmost glory and spread, showing that spring is at
the height. Ere long, the white, breaking out over
the hawthorn, will mark the transition to summer.
In the days, or weeks, during which the two
seasons kiss without parting, the beauty is exceed-

ing. At no other time is the earth so delightful a place to live on.

As the yellow came, so it dies, first. Then the white passes into the prevailing green of summer; after which there are no more colour masses or patches that can be seen at a distance, till the fields fade into straw or golden shades, and the woods take on the tints of autumn.

In this the showering season of the year, the hues are kept incessantly pure. These cloud masses, with their lit summits and dark defiles, resting on an ocean of vapoury haze, have retired to the horizon to give the midday hours over to the sun. In the afternoon they will come up again to wash the faces of the flowers afresh; again to roll away from the west, that their edge may be touched by the sunset.

After her morning, and again after her evening bath, at this maidenly time of the year, nature looks very fresh and charming. It is then that one falls in love with her, and never tires of looking on her face. I can imagine no greater delight —it is one I have often known, and would not willingly miss—than to turn towards the largest mass of yellow within reach, in the interval between the ceasing of the afternoon shower and the setting of the sun. The blossoms are still trembling with the drops, and the linnets have come out of their hiding from the rain for an even-song.

The yellow belongs to the whin and to the broom—not nearly so much to the whin as to the broom. The fainter glow on these knobs of hard rock is of the whin; the brighter hue, around the edges of the field, and where the sloping bank retreats from the stream, is of the broom.

The whins may burn with an intenser if lower flame to one who is near, but theirs is not a travelling shade. Besides, there are not so many flowers, and some are half-hidden away amid the dark green of the shrub. It does not scatter its energies in colour, but conserves them for other uses.

The seedling begins life by putting forth very soft three-leaved foliage. But in successive leaves the mid-lobe extends and sharpens, until it becomes a very formidable spike. Thus this innocent child of nature very early in life develops into a veritable Becky Sharp, who, " because of the spite of fortune, whose beginnings she couldn't remember, never had been a girl—she had been a woman since she was eight years old."

There must be some reason for this: there is for
everything. Becky Sharp was once an ingenuous
child. There may have been a time, also, when
whins only put forth soft leaves. Wherefore,
then, the change in the plant and the girl? "Many
a dun had Becky talked to, and turned away from
her father's door; many a tradesman had she
coaxed and wheedled into good-humour, and the
granting of one meal more." That seems sufficient
to account for the departure of the green leaves
and the substitution of the bristles; together with
the disposition not to mind whom she pricked—
indeed, rather to enjoy it, so long as she kept
herself right.

Let us suppose that the whin was driven
out into waste places, and that there it was exposed to duns in the shape of grazing cattle, and
troublesome tradesmen in the shape of nibbling
rodents. In this hard school it would naturally
acquire a certain precocity, quite shocking in
its way, to the sheltered growths of the
inlands.

Even in its present condition, it is still nibbled
by the rabbits into compact masses of all manner
of fantastic shapes. But as often as the persecu-
tion, which first taught it to look after itself, is

repeated, it concentrates its forces, and redoubles its means of defence.

The tender foliage of its days of innocence would prove the most acceptable of bites. Unless some device were hit upon to stay the spoiler, speedy extinction was inevitable. Suppose some of the plants, by reason of the hardness of the leaf, to become less agreeable ; suppose the hardness to increase until it pricked the creature's mouth. Here we have some sort of explanation of a soft-leaved plant becoming so formidable.

It may be asked why the broom did not change in the same way. Several answers may be suggested. I imagine that there is a bitterness about the broom, which makes it less sought after by animals than the sweeter-juiced whin.

I have seen cows pulling at every shrub round about, except the broom, even when the branches were so intermingled that it was a matter of some difficulty to disentangle them—just as I have seen them, with a delicacy one could scarcely have looked for in such large-mouthed creatures, picking the surrounding grass without disturbing the tall, upright meadow buttercup. Do not these same buttercups owe their name to the supposed partiality of the cow, which never tastes them if

it can help it, and the butter-producing qualities
in the milk they never enter?   Or was it the cool,
moist, fresh look in the cup that suggested this
cool, fresh name ?

One may test this element in the shrub by
putting a bit of the bark in his mouth, just as he
may discover why a cow avoids the buttercup by
chewing a bit of the stem.

Again, I imagine that the broom has not been so
long here; nor has it passed through anything like
the hard discipline to sour its temper, raise its
bristles, and put it on the defensive.   And, lastly,
the broom is not nearly so much a child of the
wastes, where the chief danger lies.

The simple distinction between the areas of
broom and whin is, that the whin frequents bare,
arid, and sandy stretches; while the broom finds
out unoccupied places, with a certain depth and
richness of soil, such as the margin left where the
plough could reach no nearer to the hedge.

Of course they cross into each other's domain.
Especially is this the case with the whin.   The
poor, though quite able to exist on what they have,
never object to a better home.   Often they are
seen to mingle their dark and light green foliage ;
their dusky, and bright yellow blossoms.   But

there are limits in the direction of bareness which the broom positively refuses to cross.

The whin covers the knobs of hard rock, and pays for its lodging by helping to keep the thin sprinkling of soil, gathered from the waste of the stone, from being blown off by the wind or washed down by the rain. Because of its tenant, the rock gets the common name of whinstone.

Long straggling roots give the whin a lot of purchase, thus making it independent of depth. So much one will learn who tries to grub it up. This habit of root-growth it may have acquired along with the prickles. In the way, where there was enough of earth to strike straight down into, it became a simple necessity of existence, as soon as the shrub was driven beyond the limits of cultivation. It takes advantage of every crack to tighten its grasp.

It is a veritable fir tree among shrubs, and has much the same place and function in nature. In passing through fir forest or whin scrub, one has to watch his feet very carefully lest he trip over the exposed roots. The fall is to be avoided as either very rough or very thorny. Should the hard rock form a ridge, the fir tree and whin share it between them. Nothing is commoner than the

dull glow of whin under the deep shadow of the
fir needles.   In such a situation, with its downward
tending roots, the broom would starve or be stunted
and easily torn up.

The sandy stretch of links around our coasts is
the domain of the whin, occasionally shared by a
clump of fir trees.   Seldom or never is this area
invaded by the broom.   Round St. Andrews we
have abundance of whin, with some fir trees, but
not a single broom bush.   And this is fairly representative of similar scenes elsewhere.   The glow at
the seaside, so pleasant in the cool sunshine, so
suggestive of a day among the bents with club and
ball, is still a comparatively dull glow.   It is the
glow of whin.   Anyone who has seen whin and
broom growing together will never mistake the
one for the other.

The inland yellow is the yellow of broom.   It is
that which touches spring with masses and patches
of colour.   It is that which lights up our sweet,
fresh country-sides.   It is that which marks out
the curved line of beauty of the burns, with their
suggestions of rising trout.   It is that which
washes itself twice a day in the April showers, and
then shines out in the April sunshine.

No wildling blossoms so freely as the broom.

This generous habit alone, but for its abundance, would make it a favourite in the garden. As lief imprison a little of the sunlight, or the blue of the sea, when all that is needed is a window, or an eye to let it in.

Sometimes the hawthorn strives to cover itself with white, but it seldom or never altogether succeeds—there is generally some bare spot left; whereas the broom will not rest from flowering till every leaf is hidden away. This may well have been the bush that burned " nec tamen consumebatur." No wonder that it makes the scene so bright, and gives a character to spring.

Blossom, blossom, everywhere, until the very bees themselves are puzzled with the *embarras de richesse.* The special mechanism for dusting the insects back with pollen seems thrown away, when the very weight, as it lights, seems sufficient to bring down a yellow shower. The very atmosphere surrounding the plant, even when undisturbed, is filled with pollen rain.

The dark birds are dusted yellow as they pass out from their nests. One requires no dusting. It is probable that the head of the yellow-hammer has no other meaning than the blue cap of the chaffinch, or the light spot of the white-throat, and that the bird made no conscious selection of the spring brake for nesting. But it is no fancy that the yellow head affords it some concealment, as it sings its simple lay from the broom bush, or even amid the scantier blossoms of the whin.

One would naturally expect to find such seeming-hardy, free-spreading plants among the hills. And, even should the broom fail, after a certain altitude, because there was no depth of soil there, the whin—so habituated to bad treatment, able, through much practice, to cling on to any rock, and, through much privation, to subsist on any diet—should climb as high as other plants.

And yet both reach but a comparatively low altitude, beyond which no spring yellow is visible. Both are found sparingly at the Castleton of Braemar, some twelve hundred feet above sea-level, but do not manage to struggle beyond.

The whin is an interesting instance of a comparatively hardy shrub, that can face anything but a mountain. Its lowland companion, the fir tree, climbs away beyond, and leaves it lagging behind. In these windy regions one would imagine the advantage to lie with the lowlier shrub.

V.

THE FLOWERS OF SUMMER

FROM spring to summer lies between the fading broom and the blossoming hawthorn — through a gateway overhung by lilac and laburnum.

Neither lilac nor laburnum is native, by right of long hold of the soil, although both are so closely woven in with our earliest recollections of the season, that it is hard—to me impossible—to picture it without them.   If not found in our lists of wild flowers, it only shows how very fine are the lines that are drawn, and how strangely they are made to curve in and out.   Both grow so freely beyond the garden walls, and wander so far into the depths of the surrounding country, that

5

they seem to have as good a claim as many another
form of no older date, and which most of us
never saw.

The fenceless path through the field, by which
the children, now in their sunny-weather pinnies,
go to the farm for milk, is overhung all the way.
Never was there a brighter arch. Each alternate
tree is a laburnum, some of whose drooping
racemes come just far enough down for little hands
to reach. What a handful of flowers to get all
at once! Broom stretches from trunk to trunk,
forming a second lower yellow line.

No pathway in the country is pleasanter to me
than that. I have gone up a thousand times,
morning and evening, just at this season. And
yet the farmer, who shares the charm in larger
measure than others as he drives up and down in
his gig, has of late been shaking his head.

"Unwelcome intruders into his domain," he
calls what was there while he was yet in his
cradle; and, shutting his eyes to escape the glow,
lest it might touch him, he breathes out threaten-
ings and slaughter.

"They keep the sun from his grain."

He always looks in the morning or afternoon,
when the shadow is half across to the next hedge.

"They rob the land along the edge of the field."

As if everyone did not know that he manures largely with old boots. Plainly, he has no belief in such close proximity between utility and beauty.

One day, when the blossom is off and there is nothing left to weaken his purpose, he will carry out his threat. Some are fearfully looking forward, while others say that his bark is worse than his bite. After that, he will have many a year to drive up a bare road. Serves him right! Possibly, he will not care, but that is all the more his loss.

The gateway to the farm has its summer arch. The cream of the bourtree meets the white of the rowan. Blossoms and scents mingle overhead.

The hawthorn ought to flower on the first of May, for which reason it has got the name of the month. But that is in England, where everything is earlier.

"Oh, that was past before we came away."

Such is the tantalising comment of our visitors from the south; while all is yet fresh to us, and, in the innocence of our hearts, we are pointing to the opening buds.

Our village maidens are yet simple in their
ways and thoughts, with just a lingering touch of
rustic superstition. They rise before dawn on that
magic morning, the same to-day as it was six
centuries ago.

> The busy lark, messager of day,
> Salueth in hire song the morwe gray ;
> And fyry Phœbus ryseth up so bright,
> That all the orient laugheth of the light.

In quest of dew they go forth, between hedgerows which are green as yet, to shady nooks if
they be wise. And should they gather but as
much as will wet their cheeks, the freshness of
May will be there every morning of the year.
Surely the purity of some of these complexions is
worth preserving.

With us there is no maypole or queen, or
pageant of any kind, although the children have
a game in which they dance round in a ring, to
some refrain, which sounds like a corruption of
" Merry May Day." Since dew for the cheek can
lie on the green blade, there is not the same need
of blossom for the pole. Mayhap we have no pole
because we have no blossom, and turn to the dew
as all we can get.

Be that as it may, our hedges delay breaking

into white till about the twentieth of the fresh
month; after which, for many weeks, especially
when rain-washed, they are delightfully pure and
fragrant, all over our country-sides. So that we
would willingly part with many a flower before
" The May."

The glory of summer is the hedge. The glory
of the hedge is the wild plants, which straggle,
at their own sweet will, and know not when to stay.
In such wanderers, especially of the flowering
kinds, Scotland is not very rich. Many of these
are lovers of chalk, of which we have none; and
the rest seem to prefer milder quarters.

No "traveller's joy," fitly so called, such as
lends a wealth of beauty to the waysides of the
southern counties of England, is ours. One bush
grows against a gable hard by, covering it in the
summer-time from side to side, and sending
straggling twigs away above the chimneys. And
it is hard to convince those who see it for the first
time, that such things are really wild.

No bryony breaks out of all bounds, running on
either side away from its roots, and over the tops of
the hedges. Nor does the convolvulus hang its
great white bells over the green.

And yet our hedges are not without their

charm, part of which may lie in their very reserve. They seem to make up in their sweetness for want of luxuriance. At least we don't

seem to want them to be other than they are. We have got to like them. Perhaps the only hard-wooded climber we have is the woodbine; and this is a host in itself.

The interval between the fading of the white— here we call it simply "blossom," as if there were none other to compare with it—and the reddening of the fruit is all filled up. The pretty dog-roses, tinted pink and white,

like a country cheek returning from its May morning dew bath, never lose their charm, however
many seasons old we are.   Clumps of sweet briar
are seldom so far apart as to leave any portion of
the lane unscented.

And there are vetches—yellow, blue, and pink—
which come along with the roses; and, last after
them, on to the season of the haws.   These can
climb as high as ever did "traveller's joy"; and
wander as far as bryony; and moreover have a
lightness, denied to the wooded stems of either,
and a grace beyond the great convolvulus bells.
I have seen them, clear of everything, poised
as if on their own wings, hovering over the hedges
like so many strange butterflies.

Nor can we forget such living flowers of country
lanes as the linnets, who are as inseparable from
the thought of dog-roses as the yellow-hammer
from that of broom.   I have seen the yellow-
hammer with the broom shade slightly faded, and
the linnet with the rose slightly paled, the one among
the yellow, the other among the crimson vetches.

Just as the spring shade is yellow, so the characteristic summer hues are white and blue—white
like the sunlight or the lit edges of the cumulus
cloud; blue, like the patches of the sky.   Not that

there are no other shades. Have I not been writing
of pink dog-roses? Only, when one thinks of summer after it is past, these two separate themselves
out from the rest.

Two summer blues come running ahead of the
rest. The speedwell may, or may not, be a pledge
of good fortune. That other name of veronica is
at once prettier, and more significant. It means
the true image. And all who look down upon
them must feel that they reflect the sky with
wondrous trueness. Among them there are differing shades of purity, and in some the heaven must
see itself as in a fairy glass.

There is a pretty story attached to the name,
which gives to the reflection another reference.
But in this case I shall overlook the legendary,
and abide by what is obvious and natural.

The veronicas are among the most widely spread
of our summer flowers. They grow everywhere,
can adapt themselves to any environment, accept
light and shadow with equal thanks. They are
weeds of the field and garden, root themselves
between the joints of our doorstep or the thatch
of our roof.

The common species is by the hot and dusty
roadside. The blue rock speedwell grows far above

all lower defilements, and nearer to the sky it reflects. There it is fanned by the breezes eternally playing round the mountain-tops.

Another just lifts its head above the hedge-shaded ditches and slower streams, where it is distinguishable from the white-flowered watercress only by the blue. A professional cress-gatherer—whose well-nigh soleless boots are always wet—tells me that when in leaf alone, they are gathered together by the unskilled and sold for salad.

Most deserving of the name of veronica is the germander speedwell. There the blue is delightfully sky-like in its purity. Happily, it is not rare. By roadsides with a little bank sloping up to the hedge, it grows among the springing grasses. There it gladdens the wayfarer through the fresh months of May and June, and even into hot July. I do not envy one who passes by without looking.

It refuses to be touched. When pulled, it rains down its blue flower—where all the petals are in one—to hide away among the grass. Therein it shows its good taste. It will not be taken where it cannot reflect the sky.

Forgetting the traditions of the race, one creeps in among the shades. It gets the name of mountain speedwell, though mainly found in moist woods. The whole plant is bigger. The leaf, which in the open grew close against the stem, now takes on a little stalk. Since it cannot see through the close leafage, the flower forgets the colour of the sky. The hue is pale.

The other blue is the "forget-me-not," It, too, is one of the most widely spread of our wild flowers. It, too, is everywhere,—in the gardens and fields as a weed; by the roadsides and in the woods as a wild flower; on the mountain-tops as one of our very rarest alpines. It is the very chameleon of flowers, passing through many shades in the process of unfolding. In the open flower the blue is darker than that of the veronica—more like the sky as reflected in the pool, or the blue of the wind-chased sea.

There are varieties in shade here also. The deepest and purest is that of the water forget-me-not. It grows in all sorts of moist places, nowhere more perfectly than by the grassy margin of the stream. There it can see its likeness in the pool— can dip under the flowing current for its morning bath.

Round this plant a legend has grown, with much of human pathos in it. As a play of the imagination on the natural surroundings, it is worth repeating.

A minstrel of Mayence lost his heart, and, since the poor may not marry, would go forth in search of fortune. His courage was high, if his spirit was sad; and as he bade farewell to his lady-love, he whispered her to hope for the best. Successful beyond his hopes, see him once more amid the familiar scenes to claim her for his own.

The eve before the wedding was spent in gentle dalliance by the lake-side. On an islet bank, sweet blue flowers looked coyly out from among the fresh grass. The lady sighed. In such an hour the faintest wish is law. And straightway he struck out from the shore. Strength failed him. The parting was like to come hard upon the meeting. He struggled near enough to cast the flowers at her feet. "Vergiss mein nicht," he cried, and sank.

These flowers of the air, the summer butterflies, like flowers of the land, are white and blue: white in the sunlit open country, blue near the blue sea.

Since last I watched the children on the way to the farm for milk, time has moved on a few weeks with the consequent changes. The pinnies have been through several washings, and the sprig upon them, so fresh looking on that early summer day, is faded. Hands, face, and in some cases feet also, show signs of exposure. The fair are fern-tickled, as they call it, from the likeness of the blotches to the spore-cases on the back of the fern ; the dark are brown as mulattos.

The lane, too, has changed, and at first sight does not seem quite so attractive ; at least not nearly so gay. The brambles are flowering instead of the broom, and the alternate lime trees instead of the laburnum. The white-throats are busy and silent behind the big white flowers, and the greenfinch is trilling in the cool shade of the soft leaves. And what a delightful scent of lime blossom and hum of bees ! How still and warm the air ; how almost noiseless the woods, and shadowless the fields ! Is not this the very height of summer ?

Mountain ash and elder-flowers have passed into berries. An arch of honeysuckle rises over the latticing at the farm doorway. Endless roses are growing at their own sweet will, and fast lapsing back into wildness. One among the rest is yellow, the like of which I have seen with single. rows of petals, by Scots lane-sides, in the quiet country. But whether only "escapes" which had run wild, I have been unable to determine.

Then there is the lowing of kine, and the cool sound of churning butter. The dame returns with an apron full of eggs, gathered from no stale hen-houses, with their wire-netting runs; but from barn, and stable, and byre, wherever erratic hens which spend the day in the stackyard and roost on the stalls, chose to sit. The Scots grey, missing for three weeks or more, pushes her way through the hedge with a brood of thirteen chickens.

VI

MARGUERITES AND POPPIES

IN May the daisies troop on to the links, so
that golfers have often to use a red ball, as
after a fall of snow in December. In such a dainty
favourite, however, as in the case of forward but

bright children, much is tolerated that would be inexcusable in almost any other wild flower; so that I cannot recall a single instance of a golfer being out of temper, even after the loss of a second ball.

Enlarge a daisy many-fold ; broaden its yellow disc to an inch in diameter, surrounding it with correspondingly great rays, and you get, at all events in appearance, a marguerite. The common idea of the relation between the two is that of big and little sister.

Happily, the marguerites do not invade the links. Instead of a carpet, we should then have a forest of white, scarce less lovely perhaps, but more troublesome. And the same toleration might not be extended to troops of the bigger sisters.

The marguerite is not without a history—has found its way into ecclesiastical legend, is even sacred to an apostle, all of which go to show that its attractions were recognised very long ago.

We learn that in the Church of Remi, at Rheims, there exists a coloured window of twelfth-century date. St. John and the Virgin appear at different sides of the cross. The outer edges of the aureoles encircling their heads are touched or rayed with marguerites. Each open flower turns to the central figure as to a sun.

That it was simply naturalised here, seems probable. In a sense, this is true of very many of our wild flowers; only some date further back than others. When the marguerite crossed the Channel, it were hard to fix. It has the colonist's liking for the nearness of houses; and, taking into account the unlimited powers of scattering in the order to which it belongs, is seldom found far astray. It is not a woodland plant; it seldom climbs very high; it abandons the wastes to the shabbier-looking scentless mayweed.

We ask. of a true native, that it belong to mountain, forest, swamp, sea-coast, or some modification of the four; for of these, ancient Scotland, in the main, was made up. Now, the marguerite likes dry and sunny places, of which in rude times there were few. Since the soil is drier where the ground inclines, it seeks out sloping banks.

The slopes it mainly haunts are those of very recent formation. Nothing it likes better than a railway embankment, probably because of the greater dryness caused by the looseness of the soil, and the very sharpness of the double incline.

Scarcely are the navvies out of sight, than it

arrives, along with or close on the trail of the earliest grasses. Once rooted, it loses no time in spreading. It careers on its unimpeded way, through cornfield, meadow, and marsh. Mile on mile of flat country, with few signs of man's abode, save the solitary farm, or clump of cotter houses, it crosses.

With a break, where the train descends to the level of the surrounding country, it reappears beyond. Thus, during the bright months of the year, it transforms what would otherwise be an eyesore into an elevated garden—a scene of great natural beauty. We forgive the railway embankment, when it is there, for the sake of the marguerite. No other device, especially on flat scenes, would serve as well.

It is not a daisy — not a thing of the sun. Scarce would it be too much to say that it is rather a thing of the twilight. It looks, with its great open eye—large enough to catch every ray —out on the luminous dark of the summer night. Those who go forth to see find it loveliest on the softly shaded atmosphere. One who has not looked then, does not know the marguerite.

Often in my summer wanderings have I approached the banks, long after sunset, near enough

6

to catch the dimly veiled glory; nearer still, till I could make out the separate faces of the flowers, and find that not one was asleep. One night, in particular, comes back to my memory.

I had been far afield, fishing, where the stream ran between high banks of broom and whin, slackening towards the mill dam. The biggest fish lay just where the current broke in upon the still waters of the dam. The best time was just as the light became magic. For company I had white-throats and sedge warblers, marsh buntings and meadow pipits, agreeable, if only as a change from human chatter. The charm, rather than the fish, held me.

It was late when I tore myself away and started back over a rough country. I took as near a crow-line as the ripening grain fields would allow. Distant objects had drawn over them a tender veil of summer dark, too transparent for concealment.

The railway embankment was whiter than I remembered to have seen it. There, all seemed to be just awakening from the drowse of day. I approached till I could see the faint yellow discs with the great expanded petals. Had I been more tired than I was, I could not have passed by.

The bank wooed me.   I lay down on the slope.
The fair heads bent over to whisper to me.   The
light was magic.   It was like spending an hour
among the fairies.   It has seemed so ever since—
a dream of love, purer and rarer than human !

This fair flower passed through a season of
neglect.   It is not so very long, not much more
than a decade, since the marguerite was taken
notice of in Scotland.   Years had it grown on the
same banks, and in equal abundance ; but gatherers
passed by on the other side.   Nor would the plea
for a place beside the others in their basket have
been listened to.

It was known as the horse-gowan.   " Horse " is
used for all coarse overgrown things, where there
is another and daintier of the same kind.   The
gowan was the daisy ; and the horse-gowan was
fit only to be cut down with the scythe, and,
together with the national emblem—the thistle—
presented to the jackass.   It may be that some
Maud Muller picked it out from amid the confusion of green stems at the haying-time ; but that
was only her rustic taste.   It may be that some
strangers passing on horseback paused to look ;
but that was only at the pretty face.

It is quite wonderful how rapidly the æsthetic

element progresses when once it gets a start, or is affected when once it becomes fashionable. One is sometimes not unreasonably disposed to doubt the genuineness of the admiration, even when the thing admired deserves it all. The banks where it grew are invaded ; and even its great abundance, so seldom the case, is not sufficient to make it vulgar.

Rich and poor meet when there is no need for search and no excuse for competition. Coarse hands pluck it and put it into the broken jug in the kitchen. Dainty hands pluck it and put it in the shapely vase in the drawing-room, with a few grasses to give lightness. What could be more exquisite ? Where else could it be matched, were one to wander over all the summer fields ? Perhaps an edging of dog-roses ! No ! they are better by themselves. " What a pretty name too !"

As if that had not been given by people with better eyes in their heads, when it was only the horse-gowan here. One wonders how the marguerite likes it.

" And what a perfect massing and combination of two simple colours !"

As if this, too, had not been found out ages ago.

There is a disposition to laugh at the long classic

names given to flowers. This one is even excep-
tionally long. But it happens to have a meaning,
which more than redeems its length—*Chrysanthe-*
mum leucanthemum.

The former word simply means golden-flowered,
the latter white-flowered. The two together say
" the white and golden flowered." What could be
simpler and more expressive than this? It is no
more than a description of what one sees, such as a
child might give—the white rays, the golden disc.

More refined than horse - gowans, more poetic
than ox-eye daisy, it only yields in sweetness,
though not in expressiveness, to marguerite.

The rage is, perhaps, not so great as it was; that
is only what one expects of all such sudden fancies.
The love of change is universal, and prevents one
favourite reigning for many seasons with those
who, without inherent tastes, affect what others
admire. But nothing can ever again wholly close
the senses against the unadorned loveliness of this
flower. Many will continue to visit its haunts,
and bring it back with them to purify and beautify
their rooms.

The main association in my mind, between the
poppy and the marguerite, is their common preference for a railway embankment. Sometimes

they grow together.. The red mingles with the white in nature's own unstudied way, which never errs on the side of bad taste. Sometimes poppy and marguerite divide the space between them, and even choose different embankments, as if each wished its own share of admiration; so that one train may speed through poppy-land and another through marguerite-land. Not only does the poppy appear before the marguerite, but it lingers after; and then we get a reign of pure white, and another of pure red.

Poppies do not mass like marguerites. However many—and often they may be gathered in dozens without moving from the spot—they are scattered among, and separated by the grasses.

The wanderer in the summer twilight they do not lure from the same distance. They cannot send a signal so far. One must cross the paling before he knows that they are there, and then the charm begins to work. One must kneel among them to catch the dusky glow, and the shadows lurking within the crimson lids. They are no longer pale but dark-eyed beauties, with a witchery more subtle and all their own. They are said to lull mortals to sleep. Many at least have been known to go to sleep while they watched—I

among the rest—and have suffered no evil fate,
such as they would not be willing to dare again.

Unlike the marguerite, they rebel against being
taken from their haunts. They will not be
abducted and carried over field, fence, and burn,
whether they will or no, and petted and enslaved
in a vase. They break away at the crossing of the
dyke, shake their petals free during the leap over
the ditch, or the stumble on the boulder; and all
that appears at the end is that which raised them
from the ground. Of gipsy birth, and bred in the
open, they pine within the walls.

There is no pleasanter feature in modern railway
management than the encouragement given to
good taste. This goes a little way to redeem the
frequent vandalism which offended the æsthetic
sense of Ruskin, and to soothe the irritation of
those who would have the rarer haunts of nature,
with their wild creatures and wild flowers, left
undisturbed.

Stations, which were wont to be such ugly
breaks, are now more or less bright with gardens.
Nature has done the rest—has taken charge of the
track, and changed raw piles of soil into flowery
ways.

But there are limits in this direction. Nor, for

the benefit of lazy tourists, should fresh scenes be
needlessly invaded, in the hope that the eye will
get accustomed to the outrage; and, in time, the
unsightliness will be hidden away under the white
and crimson robe of marguerite and poppy.

When the chrysanthemum leaves the railway
embankment, it follows the dry compact turf in
search of some natural slope to scatter down.   It
pauses on the edge of the fields to hail its golden-
haired sister over the heads of ripening grain.

The poppy parts with its fair companion at the
fence and takes another way.   Turning aside from
the turf, it crosses the dyke, or passes through the
hedge among the corn.   There, in the later weeks,
we shall find the crimson glowing against the
straw colour, and gaily floating on the shadow
billows, along with the golden-haired sister of the
chrysanthemum.

VII.

THISTLES.

THE thistle belongs to the later summer, when the whites and blues are already beginning to pass into the reds and purples. It is well on for the end of June before I notice the children—a little browner, a little more freckled, with evident signs of mending on their pinnies—under the lime tree getting at the cheeses. Tearing off the outer wrapping, they expose the white cushion, on which the purple-robed flowers sit in such dainty state; and this they consume, with the relish of epicures of nature.

What skilled botanists of a practical sort these children are! It is wonderful how they know what to eat, when it should be sought for, and where to find it—lessons which, as we grow up and lose our freshness, we forget more and more. On the early morning of another day, they start the hare

from her form, and the lark from her nest, in their
search for the earth nuts. They know under
what plant to find them, and how far they are
down in the ground. See them cross to the burn-
side, where they can make a salad out of the
sorrel growing on the bank.

Nor is their skill by any means confined to the
plant kingdom. On one of the thistle heads a
" foggie "—distinguished among the bees by his
browner shades and the suppression of the black
and yellow bands—is hanging. It is plain that he
is in the helpless plight of one who has partaken
too freely of the heady juices. No haste is made.
No precautions are taken for the capture. He is
not likely to fly away.

With pinnie-protected fingers the thistle head is
severed from the stem. One takes off the purple
from the cheese, while another, in a rude and blam-
able but effective way (which will occur to those
whose blessed privilege it has been to spend their
childhood in the country), extracts the honey.

Thus they, whose mothers can afford little more
than bare necessities at home, find a table of
dainties, inexhaustible in its variety, spread for
them in the wilderness.

All the way cheeses grow under their purple

flowers, with foggies here and there in addition.
And the gourmands sit down to feast under each
second lime tree. Not every thistle they come to
suits their purpose. That prickly small-headed
specimen in the ditch is of no use; that pale-
flowered fellow among the oats still less so. In
that strip of wood to the right grows the melancholy thistle, tall, unbranched, prickless. But these
youngsters are not melancholy—at least not to-day,
—and do not turn aside to see.

They pause before the great cotton thistle,
growing in front of the farm window, with much
the aspect of a small company of Liliputians
staring at Gulliver. But it is not to admire,
only to wonder what edible use it could be
turned to.

Was it John Leech who once depicted some
London street boys, small by reason of age and
hard living, contemplating a six-foot sentinel in his
box? And when the object of so much attention
was flattering himself that he had made an impression on their youthful minds, one said to the other,
" What a jolly jack-in-the-green he'd make!" Had
these children given audible expression to their
thoughts, they would have said, " What jolly cheeses
it would make!"

The thistle, which is thus only a cheese-bearer to the undeveloped patriotism of these children, is the symbol of Scotland *par excellence*. It is supposed to bristle all over with the national spirit. The prickles, which the little fingers crush with their pinnies, illustrate, if they did not suggest, the proud motto, " *Nemo me impune lacessit.*"

Altogether, there is a softness about it which belies its warlike aspect, and convicts it as a bit of a braggart. Its pulpy stem, albeit four or five inches in diameter, barely succeeds in holding it upright. A cut with a thin walking stick would double it up, and level its pride with the ground.

Nevertheless, he is a buirdly chiel, and there is much in his look to warn the timid—who do not know him so well as these children do—from trifling. No would-be Scotsman of foreign extraction, north for a fortnight's holiday, is satisfied till he has a tin effigy pinned to his newly-acquired Glengarry bonnet. Possibly, he owes part of his respect for the reality to the fact that he has made its acquaintance while masquerading in his brannew kilt.

All this presupposes that the thistle is so pecu-

liarly Scots as to lend a certain appropriateness to
its adoption ; and, moreover, that there is only one
thistle, or at least one with some unquestionable
predominance over the rest.   Neither of these pro-
positions is wholly true.

Scotland is a hilly country, and the thistle does
not take so kindly to climbing as it ought to do, if
it were to the manner born.   It is when he has
donned the kilt, as I have already noticed, that
the foreigner affects the thistle ; which is a mistake,
either in costume, or natural history, or both.   If
he were better acquainted with the modern Highlands than he seems to be, he would probably
know that the two things he is least likely to
see there are thistles and kilts.   Indeed there
are very few prickly plants among the hills,
which may be one reason why kilts used to be
worn.

In describing a Scot of the proper sort, Sir
Walter says—

> Right up Ben Ledi could he pass,
> And not a sob his toil confess.

So far from being able to climb Ben Ledi, I
question if the thistle reaches much above a thousand feet ; that is scarcely the height of the whin

or the broom. It has certainly no representative among Scots alpines, which are the true highlanders among plants. The nearest mountain relations are the blue sow-thistle and the saussurea: neither of which, despite the name of the former, is a thistle. It belongs to the plain, to the watercourse, and—be it whispered in the ear—to the rubbish heap. Even there it is very much of a weed.

Moreover, there are many kinds in Scotland, all possible or actual rivals. There is the pale-flowered field thistle, which indicates poor land or bad farming, or both, and usurps the ground rightly belonging to oats. Indeed it impoverishes much more space than it seems to cover, since it creeps in all directions under the ground with those insidious stolons. I always suspect creeping plants. They come from hungry places, and have immense appetites. We shall meet them again, and generally with the same sinister meaning. Some of them have their place in nature, covering places where nothing else would grow, and doing work they alone are fitted for. Least of all countries could Scotland do without them. But this is not one of the useful kind.

Then there is that other, lighting up the ditch
with the brilliant crimson of its flowers, whose
haunts, as in this case, are in watery places, where,
as a rule, it can do little harm.   It is at once the
fiercest-looking and the softest of the whole—a not
uncommon combination.

The lance-leaved thistle of waste places—that
cellar of the foggie, and larder of the children,
giving meat to the one, and drink to the other—
follows.   And a round dozen more, not so generally
known.

Three at least are claimants, each with its
greater or less number of clansmen.   One of them
is the cotton thistle, before whose eight or
ten feet, as it towers above the farm window,
the dwarfed children stand.   To the wanderer
in out-of-the-way places it must be familiar
as growing, during the late summer and into
the autumn, in front of many of the cottages,
·far beyond the eaves of the thatch.   I brought
a seedling from such a place, which the first
year grew to a sturdy plant.   The second season
it threw out great arms with many flowers,
and shed seedlings . enough to fill all the gardens in the neighbourhood.   A stalwart Scot, it
has much to say for itself in the matter

of height.   One looks curiously around for
the thistle   which would   presume to dispute
with it.

As if for contrast's sake, the second claimant is
a dwarf.   With no stem at all, it simply spreads
a bristly rosette over the surface of the ground.
This may be only a stunted form of one of the
rest.   If it be not, then I have not come across it
in Scotland, although I often see a thistle—chiefly
of the marsh sort—when half starved, very dwarf
indeed.

Common sense entered the judgment-seat in the
person of the late Professor Balfour.   It stands to
reason, that a thistle, chosen from the others as the
national emblem, must be that which is known to
the greatest number.   The question thus reduces
itself into which is the commonest; and there can
be no doubt that to the lance-leaved thistle belongs
the honour.

That depends on the position of the observer.
To the crofter it might be the cotton thistle; to a
son of the marshes, a marsh thistle; and to a
farmer who was still more a patriot, if such there
be, a field thistle.

There are suspicious indications, moreover, that
this thistle has spread out from the neighbourhood

of houses. It has no special habitat, no division of
the land which owns it and gives it a name. It
belongs not to the hills, nor to the woods, nor to
the marshes, nor to the coast. It has possession of
all sorts of recent heaps, and may at no distant
date have been introduced. Very probably it is
not our native thistle, in the ordinary sense
of having been longest in possession. The
marsh thistle leads a wilder and more independent life.

But common sense has something more to say
than that. The man who first gave the plant
its national significance may not have made
such fine distinctions; probably he did not. Each
prickly thing may have been to him a thistle,
and all thistles alike. Botanists, besides being
scarce, are not disposed to symbol-making, but
rather to species-making. With all their virtues
they lack imagination; and who knows how many
species have been made since Scotland first uttered
her prickly motto?

The inventor may even have called this a
land of thistles, in tones of contempt. To
whom some perfervid patriot, in a moment
of forgetfulness, may have sharply rejoined,
"Hands off, then!" Some probability is lent

7

to this supposition by the undoubted fact that the first thing even a Scotsman does is to cut down everyone he meets, which is rather scurvy treatment of anything so sacred. Certainly, I never met anyone who would not be extremely glad to see the back of every thistle in the land.

Ninety-nine out of every hundred in the present day are not botanists. Must we deny to so large a majority the right to use the patriotic symbol until they have attended classes and determined to which species they refer? Fiddlesticks! The point is in the prickle. Imagine posing an Irishman with the question, Can you point out the special clover known as the shamrock? Or an Englishman, Which rose do you swear by?

Plainly, all this pother has been raised by species-mongers. In the absence of any other, the genuine Scots thistle is the first one comes to. Its claim rests on the more or less emphatic enunciation of the motto, "*Nemo me impune lacessit.*" If we have any preference, it is for the most bristly-looking.

VIII

IN THE WOODLAND

I IMAGINE that the woods round about are old. They show every sign of being mere patches of a woodland of much greater size,—covering the whole space they mark out,—and were probably left on the less promising spots, mainly bare and exposed ridges, when the rest was broken up into farms. Many of these patches are still joined at the corners, and zigzag about in a manner which will admit of no other explanation.

Very curiously shaped some of these farms are, as they run in and out among the trees in a game of hide-and-seek. One part is cut off from another by an intervening strip, which the ploughman or the reaper must skirt or cross. So closely are some of the fields invested, that in broken seasons the farmer finds it hard to get the grain to ripen, until it is so late in the year that the sun only shows his face above the ridge for two hours at midday. Sometimes he is fain to cut it down for green food.

The age of the wood is shown in several ways, chiefly by the trees. The backbone, so to speak, is Scots fir. One half-expects this from the ridgy nature of the ground, and the bareness of the soil, which help to account for any trees being left at all.

The rest is mainly oak. Let no one suppose these to be of the brawny or spreading kind, out of whose giant trunks battleships were wont to be made. Such are not Scots oaks; at least, not those that share old woods with the fir trees. Straggling growths are these, suffering from poverty beneath, and shooting up their starved and lanky length in search of the upper light and air.

A few beech trees touch the sombreness with their fresh spring green. Though not perhaps to the manner born, or so ancient in their date, the beeches of our Scots woods more than hold their own. They grow to even greater size than the oaks, or carry more width along with their height. Than their shining trunks nothing statelier is there. Scots rooks select the branches for their nests.

Ash and poplar are more in the open, and run along the lanes which join the wood patches.

Under the fir trees, the under-growth is whin. Where the beech tells of deeper soil, the broom flowers, though less freely, and with more appearance of leaf, than out in the sun.

The floor, too, is tell-tale: it is rude and unkempt. No one ever planted a forest there. The site is elevated, reached by a sudden rise of several feet from the river. It is really a moorland stretch, in a shallow depression of a chain of hills, whose summits are about three miles away.

No soft wood-meadow grasses grow here; the hard yet graceful waved-heath grasses are a little more silvery of hue than those of the open; that is, in so far as there is room for grasses of any kind, amid the blaeberries and other moorland and mountain shrubs.

These woods of fir, with their mingling of oak and sprinkling of beech, and their rude undergrowth and carpet, are typical of Scotland.

The patch I most care for is two miles away, and involves a climb of another two hundred feet. It has a further mark of antiquity in its name. It is called "The Emmocks," probably the wood of the ants. A cart-road, marked by two running streams down the wheel tracks in winter, and scarred by two dry stony channels in summer, leads up the face of the ridge.

Why the farm at the top was called Balmy-down, no casual visitor could ever find out. But those who knew the scene best, and loved it most, guessed that it must have been christened on one of these summer days when it plainly suggested its name; that is, if the word means what it seems to do, which I by no means vouch for.

Looking down over the grass park, or the whispering heads of the wheat to the stream below, and beyond to the picturesque patches, whose wounds time had healed, cool in their firry darkness, and relieved by touches of soft green, the natural eye, aided by some association, could scarcely seek for anything more fair.

The cart-road passes behind the farmyard, and leads along the crest of the ridge to the wood, some half a mile beyond. At one time, no doubt, all this was shadowed by trees. The path-side vegetation still bears traces of the ancient state of things; for it is a long time before the natural growths can be entirely rooted out, and the rudeness refined away.

A dry-stone dyke separates the wood from a

road which has been cut through its midst. Long
enough time had passed for nature to soften and
level the top, under a layer of turf, woven of
rare moorland grasses, over which dainty panicles
danced. The curious among the woodland plants
leapt up where they could see both ways, and so
an ungainly fence was made into a linear garden
of wild flowers. To step across is to be with
nature. One finds himself under tall, graceful,
silver-barked birches. The birch is accommodating. In exposed situations it can shorten itself,
and yet remain the chief ornament of its rude,
rocky, and elevated sites. The fir hard by is
gnarled and twisted by the storms which sweep
the mountain - side, though often intensely
picturesque and characteristic in its way. The
willow becomes stunted, and takes refuge in lowli-
ness; the birch clings and cowers with feminine
grace—or when a woodland tree, as here, it can
lengthen itself in competition with the tallest,
until its topmost branches emerge into the upper
air and light, even beyond those of the statelier
beech, and all without losing aught of its proportion. The oak has struggled up, too; but what
an overgrown, long-drawn-out gawk it looks in
comparison!

The wood floor is distinctly moorland—more so even than that of the patches farther down. To the waved hair grass has been added the ruder, stiffer—altogether less graceful—mat grass. The moorland shrubs, too, have been considerably increased. In addition to the blaeberry, common to all the woods, I can gather the rose and white flower of the cowberry, and, here and there, the purple vase of the crowberry.

Quite a jubilant shout summons me to the back of the wood, whither my companion has gone foraging on his own account. I find him lying all his length on the ground, gazing intently at something. It is quite an unconscious tribute, and all the more eloquent on that account, since he did not know what he was looking at, only that it was beautiful.

Twining in and out among the shrubs are certain pink branches, at first sight scarcely distinguishable from the blaeberry twigs, except from their habit of running long distances along the ground, instead of standing more or less erect in compact bushes. Every here and there, from these recumbent stems, rises a flower-stalk, suspending, some half a foot in the air, and clear above the blossoms of surrounding shrubs, two of the

most delightfully shaded and shaped bells imaginable.

There is no mistaking this flower for a moment.
No other approaches it in exquisiteness, except,
perhaps, that second moorland plant, the bog
pimpernel, and that only from a great distance.
It is that which awakened the enthusiasm of the
great botanist, and after him was called *Linnæa
borealis*. Its presence is another sign of age. It
is not uncommon in Scots woods that have been
undisturbed. If only occasionally noticed, that is
because it is so easily overlooked, even when in
flower, by the unobservant. We swear a vow of
secrecy over that *Linnæa*, because we know that
many would be glad to take it away.

The trailing willow is all over the floor of the
wood, lighting it up with its long yellow male
catkins. A great space is beautified by the
mountain globe flower, found in these patches, and
not again till the mountains are reached. It is the
largest, and certainly the most graceful, of our
yellow wild flowers, with great soft balls of loosely
incurved petals, as big as the closed hand of a
lady.

At least four orchids grow in this wood—among
them the rose-coloured, sweet-scented orchid, and

that other with the black spots on the green leaves.

Moreover, the floor is inlaid all over with patines of bright silver, relieving the shades by countless stars. No flower, wild or cultivated, has the simple purity of the wood winter green.

Many of these, and more I could mention, are found all over the sub-alpine region of the hills, which extends upward for the first fifteen hundred feet.

The wood is a delightfully cool wood; that is the charm of it. It is worth climbing the ridge and getting heated in the July sun, just to plunge into it. It is like a water bath on a hot day, only infinitely more delicately tempered. It is not the shadow alone. Every wood has a shadow, and yet there are days when they are not cool. It is the moisture that is never absent from the air. Part of the floor is mossy and spongy. In winter one goes over the ankles there, and even in the height of a warm summer one always wets the sole of his boots.

These grey marshy stretches are relieved by the bright crimson and rose of the two louseworts, and diversified by the flat wan leaves of the butter-wort. There, too, rise the wax-like spikes of the

round-leaved pyrola. Thus, these fir, beech, and
oak trees cover over what, if exposed, would appear
as moor and marsh, and be found to contain a
fairly exhaustive representation of the characteristic flowers of both. The sundew is the only notable
absentee.

The creepies of the gipsies, or, rather, tinkers,
are visible on a bare place among the under-growth.
These not altogether uninteresting survivors of a
previous condition of existence, seem to have a
partiality for the old woods. Their knowledge of
the country is enviable, having been handed down
from generation to generation. Many a hint have
I got from seeing them turning up a pathway
which seemed to lead to nowhere. I marked that
way out for future investigation.

The donkey is luxuriating on the richest grass
he can find, with an asinine contempt for absent
thistles and present whins. Your donkey is an
epicure, whatever people may say ; and if he sometimes eats coarse food, it is because he is a
philosopher as well, and takes what he can get
without grumbling. By what sweet stream-sides
and in what cool glades have I seen the gipsy's
donkey grazing, while ordinary donkeys had to
content themselves with the sparse dust-covered

grass by the roadside. What an innocent face he
has, almost touching in its rude gentleness!

"Poor Neddy! Poor Ned!" Open-mouthed, the
gentle animal rushes at the well-meaning intruder,
who is extremely relieved when he gets beyond

the reach of his tether. Moral: Never trifle with
gipsies' donkeys.

Just beyond the creepie the floor descends into
a little cup, completely isolating one, even from the
life of the surrounding wood. No fellow-loiterer
can see down until he comes to the edge, and even

then, he finds it hard to peer through the screen of branches. Unless he hears the voices, he may pass on, unaware that anyone is there.

In the centre of the cup, the autumn and winter rains form a pool, which persists through all but the driest summers. An accommodating willow has stretched a gnarled branch over the pool, whence, in comfort and safety, one can watch the water-beetles coming to the surface and bearing down with them their silver globule of air. From just beyond the wood comes the low of kine, and in the most out-of-the-way corner of the world nestles a farm, where lives a farmer's wife, who is seldom without, and never refuses, fresh milk and floury scones.

A month later, when all these waxen flowers have given place to berries, black and red, which happily occurs at school-holiday time, children's voices are heard in every part of the wood. Tired at length the young berry-hunters, with blackened faces, gather on the willow, and chatter among the branches like so many starlings or monkeys.

And when the sun begins to dip they fill their baskets, and leave only the lessening echoes of their retreating voices to die into the silence of the wood.

IX.

ON THE LINKS

TO those who sail, or walk along, our coast
presents three phases: the cliff, the seaside
moor, and the links.

The moor differs from the links, in that it
usually has a considerable proportion of some
darker deposit among the blown sand. Those
with which I am best acquainted are near the
mouths of rivers, and may have been formed of

the mud brought down by the current, when the volume was much larger.

The three bear quite distinct wild flowers. Though directly facing the rude sea, the cliffs have still many ledges; and niches so cunningly placed as to be shut in from almost every wind. There they gather a comparatively rich soil out of their own decay, on to which seeds fall. In this way are formed little gardens, often of rare forms, worth risking one's neck to see.

The moor is open from end to end to every wind that blows. There are no corners formed by jutting points, where delicate wild flowers can hide. So much is included in the very conception of a moor—not in the sportsman sense of a shooting ground, but in that of a flat expanse, laid down under such conditions as to make it interesting to the artist, the naturalist, and the wild bird.

Still, by reason of the darker deposit among the sand, it not only affords richer food, but also retains more moisture. And there are generally marshy spots to add to the interest, and still further to vary its plant as well as its animal life.

Examples occur, all in a row,—a somewhat unusual sequence,—on the East Coast, south of Lunan Bay. Cliffs run along almost to Arbroath, and the mouth of the Tay. And such cliffs! Sheer down to the water below, or ploughed into gorges by some stream; or picturesque by reason of the outliers, cut off by the water in their retreat. Cliffs—not stupendous, but breezy and exhilarating, and with every element of natural interest.

From the Tay to the Eden, filling up the whole space between the estuaries, and possibly partly formed by the silting process referred to, lies Tents Muir. Beyond the Eden run the two miles of golf links, the length of St. Andrews.

Anyone who wishes to see what the three phases of our coast have to show—where each is of considerably more than local interest—could not do better than spend three summer days between Red Head and St. Andrews. I have spent, in each of the three, many days I am not likely to forget, and feel in a position to advise.

Unlike the cliffs, the links have no sheltered niches. Unlike the moor, they have no dark deposit. They are made up of pure blown sand. Therein consists their excellence for golfing uses; seeing that the rain so rapidly runs away; those who play on inland courses will understand what I mean. But as life-supporting areas or wild gardens, they demand, on the part of the plants,

8

that they be easily satisfied, and able to make the most of what there is.

On the sea side of the links, shutting out a view of the water from the players, is a row of the most picturesque sand-dunes imaginable. Beginning as round mounds, these have been worn into various shapes; and, in certain conditions of the atmosphere, present very weird effects.

A breezy day must be chosen for watching the growth of the young sand-dunes; and a very curious study it is. Seated on the leeside of some maturer pile, exposed to the attentions of late-building coast-birds, the situation has a certain rude charm. Borne on the wind, the blown sand eddies or swirls round the infant mounds, before it comes to rest on their flanks or summits. With every gale, the process is renewed, swelling the bulk and height of the mound. After a while, when the pile is about on a level with the rest, and may be said to be finished, the busy winds begin elsewhere.

Then the great lime-grass and rushy wheat-grass take possession, and net-work it with their hidden stems, until the surface of light blown sand becomes almost as hard as inland turf. This is the beginning—the babyhood, if we may apply the term to anything so rude — of the life of the links.

Thus, these compact dunes, besides presenting a miniature mountain chain to that exceptional golfer who has an eye for anything but his ball, serve the more practical purposes of preventing drifting over the links, and farther inland, to the detriment alike of golf and agriculture; they also prepare the way for the richer turf behind.

It is interesting to notice how many flowers can grow on pure sand. No doubt, after a while, the roots of the grasses form a certain superficial soil, varying in depth as one proceeds from the sea margin to the fence which marks off the links from the fields.

Imperceptible in the dunes, where the lime-grass seems to find sufficient in the sand for its broad brittle leaves and long stout stems, it appears just beyond as a thin streak, and deepens, it may be, to an inch in the older parts of the links. In replacing turf, the course-keepers sprinkle soil underneath; thus artificially increasing the depth.

But the layer is never very deep, and nowhere gets beyond the tawny hue, mingled of yellow and brown. The main condition of these links wild flowers growing, is that the sands cease the

restless motions of the open sea-coast, and be
brought to anchor by the stolons of the lime.

I have already spoken of the whins, which burn
with their yellow flames, through so many of the
earlier months. Some of them rise into bushes,
branching out above several feet of bare stem;
while, on the ruder parts of the links, others are
contented to lie along the ground. Ought I to
speak of two species?

No whin grows on the coast-side of the dunes;
nor on the dunes themselves, so long as they are
bare and exposed; nor anywhere, on unanchored
sand. But just within the shelter they thrive
marvellously. So far from being starved and
dwarfish, they are beyond the ordinary height
and robustness. As in the case of the almost bare
rock, they feel along the surface for any soil there
may be.

The unbroken sheet of daisies which puzzles the
golfer, does not spread so near the sea. It belongs
to the older part of the links, where the turf has
been changed more than once. The wild flowers
proper of this scene must be sought for on
the rougher belt between the daisies and the
sand-dunes, where there is less suspicion of
tampering.

The links can be very attractive on a July day. They are warm, but not so hot as the sand; their green covering keeps them pleasantly cool. No glare rests upon them. Mark out a little patch, and you will see the reason why. Look at the countless lights and shadows, due to the grass blades,—to every lit blade a shadow: the intenser the light, so much sharper the contrast and darker the shadow.

With this miniature as guide, glance over the whole, and see how mystic lovely it is. You hardly know whether to describe the effect as shaded light or lit shadow. Under the mounds the shadows gather; toward their tops the light increases. From the woods to the links, the change seems greater than it is. In the one the shadows are massed, well marked, sometimes almost unbroken; here they are in fairy lines and panicles.

Not only is there light, but colour as well. Now we have mass, more than in the woods. The colour is inlaid on the green. From a little distance it seems a glow rather than a growth, born of the air and not of the earth—a reflection from above rather than a flower bank. This is due to the shortness of the stem, scarcely sufficient to raise the flower above the sand. Everything goes to colour.

It were hard to tell which flower forms the largest patches. The light purple or pink of the thyme seems to be everywhere. Not a bank on which it does not grow. What a wild natural smell it has ! Not a namby-pamby garden smell— not a sweet sentimental odour.

There are none such, if we except the faint cocoa-nut of the whin by the seaside—no perfume proper. Such would be out of place ; the scene is too rude. It would be like scent on a ship captain's handkerchief. It smells of the breeze. Imagine the salt breeze scented—of the open—of the bank. Wilder still, only slightly harsher, is the scent of the pink restharrow.

The lotus—children call it crowfoot, or craw's taes—comes next. Not tall as under the hedge, or medium - sized as by the roadside, but with its crimson buds and yellow flowers hugging the ground.

Near the lotus, and almost as common, is its purple cousin, with the same butterfly - shaped flowers, the milk vetch. Whereas the lotus is found everywhere, this is one of the forms which, after leaving the coast, we shall not meet again

all over the plain, and until we have climbed
a little way up the mountain slopes. Under the
most favourable conditions for growth, the flower
is large in proportion to the stem and leaf. Here
it seems all flower together, quite top-heavy with
blossom. One must look carefully before he dis-
covers the delicate leafage.

The common bedstraw forms other large patches
of yellow. I have noticed that, when growing inland, and there is no commoner roadside form, the
flower has an extremely pleasant, if somewhat
wild, odour. There it shares with the white clover
the function of scenting the summer day. Here
the sweetness has departed, while the wildness
remains, and is intensified.

It is not easy to explain this deficiency in seaside plants. Where sight fails, scent is supposed to
act as a second guide to the insect in search of the
plant. It may be more needful, where the luxuriant
leafage of inland scenes hides away the colours, or
where the plant is playing bo-peep behind the
hawthorn hedge, or has retired several yards
within the shadow of the wood, or is nestling
under the steep bank, than on a flat scene
of bare vegetation and profuse blossoming.
No insect with half an eye could miss the

glow on the links, especially flying over it as they do.

There is also abundance of the delicate little white bedstraw, not quite so self-assertive, but even pleasanter to look upon.

Harebells are, of course, abroad in their favourite haunt—short-stemmed like the rest. Perhaps also a little paler in shade. At the seaside there is a tendency to part with colour as well as scent, partly from the bleaching influence of the air, and partly because less will serve to attain the end in view.

Many other plants are there whose names it would be tedious to mention. All that seems necessary is to point out the general conditions of that scene, midway between the seaside moor and the open coast, and to indicate those forms which, while they refuse to grow among the restless sand, ask no more than that the sand shall be moored by the grass roots, and so brought to rest.

Not the harebells themselves, not the scent of wild thyme, not the many-shadowed links, not the salt breeze, nor the sea, nor the whispering gush of water, is so delightful in these July days as the blue seaside butterflies. They are the veritable Ariels of the scene, appearing for a moment, then

mingling with the blue of the sea or vanishing
into the blue of the sky—returning to light on
the grass blade, and straightway, by the simple
closing of their wings, becoming once more
invisible.

X.

THE PATH THROUGH THE CORNFIELDS

THE children are sitting under a lime tree, spelling out the time of day on a dandelion.

By the way, they call it dentelion—dent-de-lion —a relic, it is said, of the old friendship between the French and the Scots, just as the sorrel at Craigmillar left by Mary's vanished hand recalls a still closer tie.

Concerning that, of course, they know nothing, and care less.

" One, two, three, four."

The puffs are very gentle, because they have to get a good deal out of it.

"Five, six, seven, eight."

After this they scarcely breathe lest they scatter too many at once.

" Nine, ten, eleven."

Quite a circle clings round the edge, needing a good strong blow from a little distance to clear the disc. The ruddiest and likeliest of the band is chosen for the final effort, and succeeds in clearing away all but two.

"Ten minutes past twelve," they reckon.

It is really a quarter past, which is wonderfully near for such a primitive timekeeper, quite as near as most modern watches come.

Thus warned of the flight of the slower winged hours, and the quicker beat of the flock of smaller minutes, the children jump to their feet, and with a rattle of cans make off for the farm.

The purple thistle is fading. To the few perfect heads the foggies cling with a helpless indecision which fears to trust itself away, lest they take other than a bee-line home. It is with thistles as with school games; they have their season. That for cheeses and foggies has gone by.

The marsh thistle still raises itself out of the ditch, until its crimson heads, brighter than ever, are quite on a level with those of the children.

These prickless cousins of the thistles, the purple roadside centaureas—ironweeds as they are called, from the hard packing of their heads--are in flower. Of little use, and less ornament, they have no interest for the needle-eyed but eminently practical naturalists. No one who has put a centaurea in his mouth will try it again. In the main, the glory has departed. The blues and whites of summer have given place to the darker hues—red and purple—not many reds, only purples.

Harebells—a relic of the blues—tremble on autumn airs, so light as scarce to fan the children's hot cheeks. Some ring their chimes down the ditch side to the dark meadow butterflies.

One tall tuft is chiming its graceful bells to a great painted lady on the path. The children approach the bells and catch sight of the butterfly. Flowers are cast away. Cans, whose descent is made noisier by rattling coppers, roll into the ditch, and the chase begins. Most of the fun is with the butterfly, which enters on the game with the utmost zest.

With arm in readiness for action, the children pull one foot after the other. Suddenly they drop the ribbonless hat. Bit by bit they lift the broken brim to peep under. Slowly they realise that the covered spot is deserted.

" There it is ! "

And they are off in pursuit.

After a merry curve over the field, the butterfly

comes into view, and lights on the selfsame spot. The tactics are repeated a little more wildly this time. The painted lady embarks on a second frolicsome course, to return in the same tantalising way as before. And so on, until the children are fain to gather up flowers and cans and pursue their way.

The rowans are reddening, and the elderberries blackening. The woodbine is still shedding fragrance from an arch of fantastic flowers. The haws, with which the hedge abounds, are just showing a touch of colour on one side. Hips have taken the place of the dog-roses.

The big thistle is at its tallest, and sends out on all sides giant arms, bearing great pink heads. A crowd of thrushes are busy on the beam tree. A smaller band of children are equally busy on the unripe haws.

This is all they see until they are coming back. And then they catch sight of their elder sisters sauntering up the way as if to meet them, but really on an errand of their own. At great risk of falling, and to the sound of jolting milk, they strive who will touch first.

Tall in comparison with the little ones these sisters are. Some fair, some dark; neither more nor less fresh and pleasant-looking than country maidens usually are.

"See! see!" say the breathless runners, holding out what they have gathered.

There are nodding harebells, and a sprig of crimson herb robert, and a little scarlet poor man's weather-glass, got on the field side, and a whole shower of star-like stitchworts, and a bit of sweet briar for scent; and just a little morsel of woodbine which grew outside the gate, "and didn't belong to the farmer, you know : did it?"

The children have only half satisfied their elementary consciences about the woodbine, and coaxingly appeal for the approval of their elders.

"Is that all?" say the sisters discouragingly. "Look what we have come for."

They lift the little ones above the level of the tall corn, and there over the forest of yellowing grain is paradise ; at sight of which the withered and despised collections of the morning are dropped to the ground.

"You see what it is to be big," say the maidens.

And then the whole band begin to walk along the edge of the corn, the children waiting in faith below, the maidens watching above for some of those glorious things to come within reach.

A long stretch of the tallest, whose unbound
hair, as it drops from her shoulders, is of the same
hue as the yellow grain with which it mingles,
secures the first prize. This turns out to be a large
flower of a pink hue, a member of the graceful
group of the campions. The familiar name is corn-
cockle; but whether these girls have one of their
own for it, as they have for most things, I could
not catch. But, name or no name, they all agree
that it is fair as any flower of the garden; and
there is some competition among the younger
members to carry it.

A rush, and a ripple of maiden voices, tell of
another flower in sight. It is a little farther afield.
What with the competition and the impetus of the
race, the winner steps or is pushed just a foot or so
among the grain, leaving a little gap of bent stalks
and drooping heads. Silence falls on the group,
and a timid glance is cast up and down the road to
see if any of the farm people have been looking.
Then the grain is straightened once more, so that
no one could have told that anything had happened.

This is a still lovelier prize than the other.
What blue in nature can compare with the
circle of florets round the pink disc of the field
cyanea ?

Concerning the proper name of the plant, or rather the sole right to the name it sometimes gets, there is a considerable difference of opinion. One day the farmer, a shrewd man, whose keen eyes look out from beneath shaggy brows, stopped me by this very field and pointed it out as the " blawort." I was struck at the time, less with his knowledge than the evident enthusiasm of one who had a sworn feud with the laburnums and lime trees. Did not these field flowers equally bloom at the expense of the grain !

And now the verdict of these maidens, better than much discussion, is on the same side; all of which goes to show that from our blues, our borages, our bells, our forget-me-nots, this has been chosen out as pre-eminently the bluewort. Perhaps it is better known to country people than the others, or was in olden shearing days, when all were abroad during the bright autumn months.

The field is an exception to every rule, and the hues of all the seasons at their best mingle with the corn.

No excitement is manifested as the somewhat washed-out lilac of the blue-cap is added to the increasing collection. Not until a richer yellow flushes the straw-coloured grain is there another merry stampede, moderated by the remembrance of their recent transgression.

"Gowans! Gowans!" is the cry. True, they call other flowers gowans as well; in the country they have general names for similar things; but this is the true one.

Golden they are! Golden they look in the autumn sunshine and amid the paler shades! Chrysanthemums! Flowers of gold! Golden rays! Golden disc, nearly two inches across of rarest, richest gold! No need to hurry; there are plenty for all. "Far too many," says the farmer, relapsing into bad humour. But what care these heedless minds, these children of the senses, for questions of profit and loss!

Weeds are flowers in their wrong place. Pity, then, that such glorious flowers should be in their wrong place, and that war to the death should be waged against them in the interests of modern cultivation. The fields of Germany are brighter than those of Scotland. Those of the islands and other outlying parts of the land are gardens in comparison with the unbroken yellow of many of our fields.

They are not in the wrong place, as far as the fitness of their surroundings goes. Nowhere could

9

they look so well as among the grain. It would almost seem as if they were aware of this. For most of them refuse to wander, seem nervous to approach even the margin of the field, and are seldom surprised far away. If odd ones appear here and there, it is only for a season; and, being annuals all of them, no progeny seems to be left. Cornflowers appear in the wilds seldomer even than cultivated plants, and are much more reluctant to settle there.

In the gardens to which, because of their brightness, they are often transported against their will by the injudicious, they have already lost half of their charm for lack of environment. The gaiety with which they laughed among the corn, or peeped through between the heads, or rejoiced as they rose and fell on the billows of light and shadow, and hailed one another over the field, is all gone. As well take one of the village maidens and place her in a drawing-room.

Golden handfuls are passed down to the children.

But the best is yet to come—the cornflower *par excellence*, which makes the autumn fields a joy and a memory.

Poppies! Poppies!

Not wayside poppies, not shabby poppies, not

washed - out poppies, but they of the short-fruited kind—poppies with ample petals of intensest scarlet dye ; not nearly so common as many seem to think—absent from large districts of the country where poppies abound—oftenest found, perhaps, near the seaside, probably because of the poverty of the soil.

These, wherever found, are the true corn poppies. See them against the yellow, see them in the sunshine, see them in the shadow, see them in the ripples of light and shade, see them anyway, and say if ever you saw anything so fair.

Poppies are distant in their mood ; it may be because their beauty is so evanescent that a touch will dissipate it, their petals so fragile that a movement will shed them.   Hand grasps hand to prevent the yellow-haired maiden falling forward among the yellow grain.

Satisfied at length, they turn away and pass the clump of harebells chiming to the selfsame painted lady.   The butterfly rises to tempt another scamper; but the young have grown wise by experience, and the maidens have other thoughts, innocently vain, in their heads.

They sit down, big and little, under the selfsame lime tree to portion out the spoil, and to deck themselves with colours suited to each complexion.

"A poppy for you, and a gowan for you."

And a little cloud comes across the sun, and a shadow falls through the air, and a gentle breeze chases over the field, and the heads of corn bend down as if to listen to the converse of the maidens.

"And a blawort for you."

Attracted, it may be, by the murmur, some outsiders of the great flocks of linnets and greenfinches feeding on the grain come to the edge of the field, and bend the stalks still further that they too may hear.

Meantime the children have secured another dandelion.

One, two, three.

Without any act or wish of theirs, the third blow clears the disc. So quick is the passage of time in these early years ! The long shadows cast over the straw colour by the lime trees might have told them that, had they cared to look.

" It's three o'clock ; what will mother say ? "

Not that they fear ; for they know that the blame will fall on the elders.

Bright are the hats, careless the minds, and innocent the spirits of these country maidens as they pass homeward along the path between the cornfields.

XI

FLOWERS OF THE FAR NORTH

THE wild flowers of one corner of Scotland are
so exceptional in their interest, so characteristic of their haunts, that they ask to be treated
apart; especially as they are so shy at crossing
their very narrow boundaries, and are so seldom
visited in districts which offer less attraction to the
many.

The north-east dip of sandstone which forms the
county of Caithness is mainly of rough moorland,
rising very little above sea-level. It passes under
the shallow Pentland Firth, to be continued, in a
certain broken way, in the sandstones of Orkney.

This whole district, though northern, is not
highland; the climate, though on the Polar side of
us, is rather milder than our own; the wild flowers,
though boreal, are neither alpine nor arctic.

A few of the hill plants come down the slopes,

134

and make themselves at home near sea-level. This is by no means strange. Hardy mountain forms are known to grow on coast moors, chiefly such as are so rude and exposed as this. Among others the eight-rayed mountain avens — *Dryas octopetala*—appears on the flats of Caithness, and crosses to the low heights of Hoy.

Some few years ago I spent part of the summer in Orkney, under the soothing ripple of canvas. Within half a stone's-throw was a lake, constricted in the middle, and swelling out at each end, somewhat after the shape of an ancient hour-glass.

Down the slope we ran with a towel for a morning bath, and again with our rods for a forenoon's cast. As fishing sheets, the weakness of this and other Orkney lakes is the abundance of pond-weed, rising to the surface as the season advances, and covering large areas when the sport is at its height. In July and August much of the water is unfishable, and a rise too near the forest, leads to the twisting of the line round the stems by the running trout. This nuisance is on the increase from year to year, and will soon have to be dealt with.

Round the lake margin was a circlet, broken here and there, of the pink bells of the bog pimpernel. This is to the wastes what *Linnæa* is to the woods, and is well-nigh as graceful and delicately-tinted as the wild flower which seemed so charming to Linnæus. The difference in appearance may be because the one grows under shelter, and the other in such places as stunt the growth.

The colour was pale—the result, no doubt, of exposure to the sea breeze, whichever way the wind blows. Some of the bells were white. The same bleaching process appeared in the purple scabious, the crimson ragged robin, and the violet self-heal. All showed many white flowers.

The scene was unrelieved. No trees were visible. The crofters' houses, dotted down here and there, only increased the impression of bareness—they were so rude themselves.

"I very much long for trees," said one who had never left the island. "If I were not so old"—he was beyond the four score—"I should go south yet."

It seems strange how one gets accustomed to anything. After the first few days I was not conscious of the want.

Immediately round the crofts, were patches reclaimed from the universal moor. The cereals were oats, and bere—a six-rowed form of barley. These strips, sparsely covered as they were, frequently came out in vivid contrast to their duller surroundings; while, in that moist air of diffused rainbows, the dull shades themselves became marvellously bright. The changes to beauty were sudden as surprising. On the rude background of untamed Orkney, beyond the crofts, I have seen atmospheric effects like the flush of distant flowers, only lovelier and brighter.

If the crops were thus thin, the space between the stalks was fully occupied—for better or worse, according to the point of view. What was lacking in use had been given over to beauty. I never saw so many cornflowers.

The fields were simply inlaid with heartsease —not the ordinary long-stalked, small-flowered field variety of the south, scarce deserving to rank above a weed. Round as a sixpence, with space for each of the shades to come distinctly out, they were such flowers as we find on the dry short turf here, and even larger than our best.

All this would seem to show that our field violet is simply the miserable outcome of competition with the taller and stronger grain. If the hearts-ease first came here as a wild flower of cultivation, it must have been as it appears in the meadows or on these Orkney crofts, and it has slowly degenerated with improved methods.

These rude fields, thus carpeted out of all comparison, more delightfully than our own, were o'ertopped and almost o'er-canopied with gowans. Though this was doubtless owing to the bad soil and worse tillage, still it made them gardens of quite exceptional beauty. Within the dry-stone dykes, in many instances, grew elder bushes (bourtree). It seems almost unaccountable at first that such a soft-wooded bush should flourish in places so exposed and windy that not even the hardiest of shrubs has a chance. But so it is! And but for this fact the outlook from the windows of Orkney crofts would be still drearier.

It chanced one day that a gentleman farmer—or as near an approach to one as the different conditions of Orkney agricultural life permitted—passed our way. Struck with the strange phenomenon of a tent where no tent should be, and which, like Jonah's gourd, seemed to have sprung in the night, he called to see what it might mean; and before leaving he courteously invited us to return the visit at his house, some few miles away.

Two days later found us out on the search in the direction indicated; for, after three or four weeks gipsying, a little social life of the unexpected sort comes as a relief. Hidden by a plastered wall of considerable height from the passing gaze, the cottage had undoubted claims to picturesqueness.

The inmates seemed to counterbalance the desolate surroundings by a cheerful inner life.

There may have been a little philosophy in it, such as common-sense people cultivate where matters cannot be mended; but there seemed to be a good deal of nature as well.

Certainly, I never witnessed such bubbling over of animal spirit even in the brightest scenes, especially on the part of those who were no longer children. The example was contagious, which

would not have been the case had the gaiety been
forced. One could not help laughing along with
them, and he would have been very dull and ill-
natured who tried. There was wit, too. There
generally is with persons who still see both sides
of life, even when one of them is not so obvious as
it might be.

In bad weather, when the brown shades looked
black, and there was no relief anywhere, they
didn't require to look beyond the garden wall; and
like wise folk, who refuse to meet depression
half-way, probably they did not try. All of the
soaked and blackened earth they could command
from the windows, were the tops of the hills.

Within the enclosure, the scene was as if I had
been suddenly transported south again. It must
have been only so much the brighter on the
duller day, and thus helped to preserve the
balance. Garden vegetables grew to the usual
height, and were bordered by bright annuals.

In a snug corner, shut in between the gable
and the wall, where the blast would pass over
without sending down so much air as would
disturb the dust on its glass roof, nestled a little
conservatory. It was just such a spot as one
would choose out for telling a world-forgetting

story in. And, I daresay, those northern imagina-
tions sometimes used it for the purpose in the
dull winter-time.

That autumn day it was suggestive of something
milder. The retreating shelves were hidden away
amid the colours of geranium, pelargonium, and
fuchsia. All this brightness was backed by the
green of native ferns. For the presiding spirits
were lovers of nature, even more than florists.
There many a summer afternoon was dreamt
away, in sweet forgetfulness of monotony and
dulness.

The ladies were enthusiastic gardeners—indeed
must have been, to have achieved such results as
these under prevailing conditions. They trembled
between the humorous and the pathetic in their
description of the difficulties and disappointments
of horticulture in Orkney.

"It's all very well for you to admire now," said
one, half poutingly; "but if you only knew what
trouble they have been, and how much anxiety
they represent. When we have just coaxed them
above ground, and are saying to ourselves, 'Soul,
take thine ease, sleep in peace,' a south-wester
will rise through the night, and in the morning
great foam flakes are flying over the island,

crusting the garden with salt, and destroying the promise for the year."

"You have great storms, then?" I inquired.

"Storms! I should think we have," and the fun came dancing back to her face. "There are days when, if you open your mouth to the windward, you must turn round before you can get it shut again."

The idea of the wind keeping the mouth open, as it might do an umbrella, was certainly original. The only improvement were to carry the parallel further, and suggest the blowing inside out.

"But I love Orkney," she went on, with the northern light in her eye. "You are too late for the finest and rarest of our wild flowers. You say that you have never been here in the spring? Then you must come."

And she spoke with much enthusiasm of the beauty of the vernal squill; and of the delightful surprise, at the close of winter, of going out some morning when the sun was shining through and glorifying a veil of moist air, to find it already scattered far and wide over the landscape.

"You, who are so rich in wild flowers, will laugh at my innocence," she said, with an assumption of humility.

I assured her that we had nothing in the south more beautiful than the few-flowered blue lily, except perhaps its sister, the bluebell of the woods.

" And sisters don't quarrel," I added.

" No," she said doubtfully; " at least not in Orkney—there are too few of us. And we have the scilla all to ourselves ? "

" Not quite, but almost. It crosses to Caithness. Caithness, you know, is only a part of Orkney."

I put it the wrong way about, to smooth her ruffled susceptibilities.

" Well ! " she said, in a hard, questioning voice.

" It crawls down the east coast—very reluctantly, perhaps—as far as Banff."

I have since discovered it on St. Andrews links, and have little doubt that it grows on similar exposed situations elsewhere. My experience teaches me to be exceedingly suspicious of any hard-and-fast limits assigned to species. But of all this she is happily ignorant, and so was I at the time.

" Is that all ? "

" And as for the west. Why, of course it crosses into Sutherland. You couldn't help it doing that, seeing that county lies next to Caithness, without any brick wall between."

"Sutherland, does it? Any more?"

"It appears just here and there down the coast, always near the water. It never forgets that it was born of the Orkney sea breezes, and scattered over your island by the first spring west wind. It nowhere seems to meet its woodland sister, the bluebell; at least I never heard of the meeting. Your scilla is not bright blue like the other?"

"No, it is pale."

"That is because it is a child of the sea. Now, the bluebell creeps up the centre of the country, disappears into dens and other snug places by the way; shivers back from the coast unless there is abundant shelter; and positively refuses to venture into Sutherland or Caithness. Your pale seaside bell forms a sort of ring, very thin and interrupted, round the inland and woodland bluebell."

"I wonder if they really do meet anywhere?"

The idea of two sisters held apart affected her imagination, and sentiment for the moment prevailed over her common sense.

"If I hear of it, I shall let you know."

In St. Andrews they are divided only by the breadth of the town—the scilla growing on the links to the north, and the harebell in sheltered places of the cliffs to the south.

" You have missed another Orkney flower, which, but for the dryness of the season, would have been here yet. It is not so easily seen, but worth searching for, and when found worth looking at. You have no lilac primroses where you are ? "

" No. There is said to be one somewhere ; but I never saw it, or met a person who had done. At most, there can only be a few plants."

" Not our primrose ? "

" No, it is taller. Yours positively refuses to grow on our hills, although we can't tell why ; has not been found on our sheltered lowlands, and probably would be choked if it tried. It seems to belong to such exposed sea-breezy places as this. It strikes me as the Shetland pony among plants —so minute is it, so much at home in its own domain, so sensitive to change, and so perversely determined not to oblige those who would grow it elsewhere, however kind they may be."

" Long may it keep in that mind."

" I am of opinion that it owes its minuteness to the hard living; and, even if it could be coaxed into settling farther south, it would after a while begin to grow bigger. But the chances are that it would die before that came about."

10

"What a spirited little plant! I shall think twice as much of it in future. You can't rob us of that."

"Of course it crosses into Caithness, which, you know, is so very like Orkney."

"Well, I suppose I must give in about Caithness," she said, with a pout. "But why wasn't the Pentland Firth on the other side?"

XII

UP THE GLEN

ON an August day, allied to the summer gone
by in its cloudless sky and breathless
warmth, rather than to the coming autumn with
its crisper air and shaded sunlight, I found myself
in Kirriemuir. J. M. Barrie was still unhatched—
I mean in a literary sense—and Thrums had not
yet wakened from its long sleep to find itself
famous.

This was by no means the only visit. The place
has a power to draw me for a distance of ten miles
on all sides. Besides, it lies directly in the way of
some of my favourite haunts; and I must needs
pass through in order to reach them.

Kirriemuir is on the northern margin of Strathmore—the greatest, as its very name implies, and
also the quietest of Scots valleys. It is a quaint
other-worldly town—as becomes the site—of un-

spoiled folk with no more than their share of conceit in themselves. Not very long ago, outsiders of simple tastes sought it instead of some more stirring holiday resort, alike for its moorland air and soothing naturalness.

Sometimes I feel glad that I knew it in those days. The place must ever be most to those who loved it before others so much as heard of it. Whatever Kirrie may mean, muir or moor aptly enough describes the surroundings, and indeed the condition of that portion of the strath.

A short way to the north the Lowlands pass quite suddenly into the Highlands of Scotland— so suddenly indeed, that in some places it is easy to step from one to the other.

Once upon a time the strath was a glacier track, and frozen side-streams flowed out from among the hills, to join and swell the great river of ice. The path or channel of these tributaries is now marked out by just so many glens ; while all that remains to represent a volume once reaching to the mountain-tops is a streak of water running down the centre.

It was yet early morning. The cool shadows cast by the irregular buildings lay across the street, some of the taller climbing far up on the opposite side. I must have passed the little house upon the hill, then, as at other times, quite unconscious of the immortality in reserve for that unpretentious structure, and the thriving trade it was destined to do in refreshments, with those indefatigable pilgrims and hero worshippers who are determined to be disillusionised.

Which of these side glens, leading a varying number of miles into the very heart of the Highlands, was I to take? Three complete and several broken ones were available; to all of which Kirriemuir—with a possible rival in Alyth—was, so to speak, the lodge. This special morning I chose that of Clova.

The only way of getting there was on foot. On certain days a coach ran, but this did not happen to be one of them. Even had it been, it is questionable if I would have taken a seat. It was no privation. And I strongly advise those who love the Highlands, and wish their love to continue, never to get on a coach where the distance is walkable. One who has not a pair of legs, or the will to use them, should stay at home. The plague of cycles had not then broken out.

The delight of the start comes freshly up as I

write—so vividly indeed, that I shall abandon my-self to the thought that it is happening over again, and write in the present.

The hills at this point stand three miles back. As I pass over the open country the sun continues to climb higher, and the shadows shorten. At length I cross a considerable stream, issuing from Glen Prosen, and then I know that the very next valley I come to is Clova.

As one steps from the Lowland sandstones to the Highland schists, a change, like that of the strata, passes over the wild flowers. Familiar forms are missed, while others take their place and do their work. For each plant has its place to fill, and work to do; except perhaps a few gipsies, which settle on any waste piece of ground, where they are left in peace. For obvious reasons, such vagrants are not nearly so common in the Highlands.

It were long to tell everything which adds its little to the general change. Details are alike wearisome and uninstructive. Enough that I mention one of the larger, perhaps the very largest, contributors, leaving such of the rest as may strike me to be picked up as I go along.

The commonest flower of the plain is the daisy.

It is the white garment or tippet the earth puts
on to show that spring has come. No meadow or
pasture or green roadside, if the grass grow not
too rank, is without it—except it may be some
seaside moor—it loves not wild places. Nor can it
be said to care for shadow. It haunts the margins,
but barely enters the woods. And the daisy is one
of the missing flowers.

Yet one scarcely misses it. There is the same
sheen ahead ; and, as all is rude grassland together
here, the effect is so much the more widely spread.
The unobservant are not even aware that another
agent is at work; but so it is.

That other is the eyebright, not altogether pure,
touched with purple. But is not the daisy also—
" the wee, modest, crimson - tippèd flower " ? At
a distance both seem white.

The names of the two (that do the same office in
different scenes—reigning, the one over Highland,
the other over Lowland turf) are strangely alike—
days-eye and eyebright. One lifts the crimson
lids, which have been dropped during the dark, to
greet the morning, and exposes the golden ball
without blinking throughout the hot and bright
hours ; the other, from its specific name, *officinalis*,
seems to have been credited with some medicinal

virtue—probably that of adding lustre to the eye of beauty.

The eyebright is not unfrequent on the plain, but is generally found in such rude places as the daisy does not care to invade; so that their domains, though they often touch, sometimes even intersect, remain essentially distinct. Both appear on the links; but the one haunts the older and maturer, the other the younger and rougher portions. The eyebright has not the same objection to shade, and is common in the older Lowland woods.

Steady walking, without a break, is not for such a forenoon as this. It is quite a delusion to suppose that there is freshness in a Highland glen when the day is warm, or shelter when the sun is high. The rays beat down with pitiless severity; the heat gathers into ovenlike intensity; there is no gully anywhere on the investing heights deep enough to create a breath. One often sighs or gasps for the open plain, where he is at least sure of what wind there is, just as a dweller on the plain sighs for the seaside. Happily, there is always the escape to the mountain-tops.

Everywhere one is within hearing of the water, with its suggestion of coolness. But there are days when the very ripple speaks of motion; and the sense of motion begets heat.

I seldom go abroad without my rod. It serves as walking-stick or alpenstock, is convenient for pushing aside the thorns, and is ever ready to be turned to its legitimate use. I sit down by the alder, and lazily fit in the pieces and string through the line. The shadow is oppressive; the very heat seems to be taking refuge from itself under the same bush. It rests upon one with the weight of another garment. I wonder if there is more air in the open.

The bed is rocky; the stones stand out like the ribs of a lean man. The stream is broken into many separate currents, which flow in attenuated channels, and only gather here and there behind the larger boulders into triangular mid-stream pools.

One such still place, more promising than the rest, is well over to the other side. A cast may bring something.

Phew! how hot it is! And only a two-inch trout, after all the trouble! How he disappears beneath the nearest stone on being returned to the water, after his first visit to the upper air! A trout in a much-fished stream must have a lively time of it! Ten miles at this rate means ten hours; it will be cool enough then!

A few such diversions to the water-side, with the needful slipping down and climbing up steep banks, and leaping from boulder to boulder to get at some likely pool, or climbing such awkward fences as only crofters know how to put up and black-faced sheep to get over, especially when the encouragement is of the slightest, prove enough. And the face is turned a little more steadily toward the goal.

Next to the daisy, the dandelion is the most familiar of plants. The one is gathered by the Lowland girls for stringing into bracelets, the other by the boys for feeding their rabbits.

And the dandelion is being replaced by the hawkweeds. Nine out of ten of our hawkweeds— many of which have a beauty of their own—are mountain forms, the majority belonging to the Scottish mountains. A few outliers come down to the glen, and a few intermediate species connect these with the flowers of the plain.

Crossing freely from the glen to the lowlands is the pale yellow mouse-eared hawkweed. It just enters within the domain of the dandelion, and in certain neutral places the two grow side

by side. But the lemon hawkweed is found
where the orange dandelion is not, and *vice
versâ*.

On the links are a few dandelions and many
mouse-eared hawkweeds; but there they observe
much the same limits as the daisy and the eyebright. Dandelion and daisy are found consorting
on the newer, eyebright and hawkweed on the
older, portions. One reason may be found in the
long milky taproot of the dandelion and the
creeping stolons of the hawkweed. Such pro-
visions seem to mark each off for its mode of life.
While the dandelion, like the daisy, keeps very
much to sunny places, the lemon hawkweed, like
the eyebright, creeps under the shadow of the
older woods.

The common ragworts, with the unequal lobing
which gives them their torn look, are left behind.
On moist ground, the marsh species, less deserving
the ugly name because of the greater regularity of
the leaves, appears. As a rule, marsh species are
extremely accommodating.

Here and there, mainly in shady places, grows
the somewhat similar, but much more graceful,
golden-rod, with its long lance-shaped leaves and
pretty spikes of yellow flowers. This is a charac-

teristic sub-alpine form, and strikes one who
approaches the hills as something new.

The buttercups, with their much-cut foliage, are
down on the plain.   And only the marsh species,
with their usual indifference to the presence of
anything but water, care to climb.   Such are
found in moist places so far away as the arctic
lowlands, water seeming to remain the same
wherever it is found.

The distinctive cups of the glen are mainly
white; and among them is the most attractive of
white cups, alike in its perfect shape and in its
proud and graceful pose.   The grass of Parnassus
—for so runs its stately and fitting name—comes
as a revelation of unexpected beauty to those who
see it for the first time, where it grows side by
side with the bright yellow of the bog asphodel.

In Scotland I find that the foxglove, though not
unknown on the plains, affects the glens and hill
slopes up to a certain low altitude, marked perhaps by the upper limit of the bracken region.   A
favourite site is the heap of stones, representing
some ancient moraine, or piled up by the simple
disintegration of rocks.   There it pushes its way
through, together with the oak fern and the
colourless spike of the wood germander.   Or it

forms the somewhat lurid undergrowth of the thin strips of dark fir, above where the whin ventures. It seems to have much the same claim as the golden-rod to be treated as a sub-alpine.

Seaside wild flowers reappear. The mosses change; the grasses change. The stone dykes, where such there be, show a transformation of roadside forms. Among ferns, for instance, there is a lessening proportion of the common polypody, so familiar on similar old Lowland fences.

" Phew! How hot!"

The sun has passed the meridian, but the warmth has not, and I am afraid never will. A shadow rests on the sloping bank ahead—not a very long one; for at this hour of the day, at this time of the year, shadows are at the shortest.

I shall sit down for a minute or two—not more than five! Why keep bolt upright, when one can lie! As well be comfortable for the short time! This slope just fits into the back! My head is out of the glare, and I can gather my hands under it thus! What matter that my boots roast! One o'clock! Eight miles yet! Two miles an hour! Five! Just nice time! Heat and cold make one slee—!

And the shadow of that tree must have stolen,

unwatched, over my boots, and crept stealthily
across the road, while I lay in deeper shadow still.
Ere I see it again, it is already beyond the dyke
on the opposite side; there is no more time for
trifling.   The pace is now persistently forward,
though still extremely moderate, for the margin
of a summer day is large.

The common lady's-mantle grows by every dusty
roadside down below, washes its flower racemes
of dull yellow in every burn that waters the plain.·
If it is sometimes hard to see how some plants
ever got their popular names, there is no difficulty
in this case.   When held downwards by its stalk,
the leaf is a miniature of a green mantle just taken
out of its folds.

Not less familiar, by Highland pathways and
stream-sides, is the alpine lady's-mantle.   It is
often one of the first of the flowers to tell that
the dividing line between lowland and mountain
has been crossed.   In many places it carpets the
glen.   The name would seem to have been given
to the plain form first, and afterwards applied
to that of the hills.   The creases or folds have
been divided into five little leaflets, which quite
take away the appearance of a mantle.   The flowers
remain the same.   In gardens or rockeries it has

a tendency to increase the number of leaflets indefinitely.

There are ragged glens, which shoot up a majestic peak here, and are comparatively tame there. The strength of this one lies in its cumulative impressiveness. Nowhere sensational, it is everywhere calmly majestic. It gains upon the spirit by degrees, until it takes full possession. On entering, one feels that he is constantly passing on to something greater. On returning, one feels that he is being let down, so to speak, to the plain.

A few scattered houses appear, in a magnificent amphitheatre. One must concentrate his attention before he can see them, so little are they in comparison with their surrounding. There I must stay; if anywhere, under a roof. The first cottage is not promising. The door is shut, the chimney smokeless; a black-and-white pig is gardening in the front plot; the knock yields only the echo of an empty house. Never mind! the ground is dry, the heather springy, and I can sleep a mile or two farther on, in the solitude of hills.

A second application is somewhat more successful. There is a room, not in this cottage, but in some older structure behind, of whose accommodation the woman speaks with perfect plainness and a becoming modesty. I follow her to the back premises and up a narrow wooden stair.

The bed is a procrustean concern, in a very tight corner of the wall. The atmosphere is provided by six drying cheeses. On the other hand, the skylight is innocent of glass—a very distinct advantage on such a night. Possibly, much to her surprise, I say it will do. I refrain from telling her that I have put up with worse.

Half an hour afterwards I am climbing the slope. Two tarns overhead are steaming like volcanoes, with craters formed by the surrounding mountains. The day exhalations are being condensed by the nightly fall of temperature. About five hundred feet above my lodging for the night, I lie down to watch the sun dipping behind an elevated horizon, picturesquely broken by the mountain-tops; and the mystic light coming out below.

XIII

THE HEATHER

THE freshness, for which I have panted all the day, dwells up here. The tail stream from the tarn, coming out of the mist, passes about fifty yards to the right. Though its motion, as it rushes down the slope and falls headlong into the frequent pools, is so boisterous, it awakens no longer the sensation of heat, but of coolness. The glare has gone out of the light. Mountain shadows fall across the glen, as the house shadows fell across Thrum's streets in the morning.

The contrast of this evening lounge on the hill-side, compared with the involuntary siesta on the way up the glen, is great. How pleasant is the South Esk as it runs down the valley, with a margin

11

of cool black shadow under its banks! How tempting the distant ripple of currents that scarce cooled the feet at midday!

Not far off is a moist patch. Round cushions of pale sphagnum are touched here and there with red by our native insect-eater. I find that the sundew almost always chooses cushions of sphagnum, where they are to be found. It may be because these retain sufficient moisture in all states of the air; and also, that they offer a background against which it more easily catches the eye of its insect prey. There is scarcely any other white background over all its hillside or moorland haunts.

On the same marshy spot grows the cross-leaved heather, easily known by its pale downy look. From the shape of its very large flowers, it gets its familiar name of bell heather, though the so-called bells are almost closed at the mouth into little balloons.

This is the earliest of the year's heather. Pale at first, the blossoms blush on the exposed side, where they are kissed by the sun into rose; after which they swiftly fade into an unsightly brown mass. As these three stages are very often present in the same cluster, one has sometimes to search a long time for a perfect sprig of rose-and-white.

Of sprawling and somewhat slovenly habit, it presents a frequent dishevelled washed-out appearance. Under the most favourable circumstances, like many another rose-and-white beauty, it looks better at a distance.

The hue of the opposite hill-slope, extending far and wide on either side, is not rose, but purple. This purple form is the next to flower, and seems to be the only one some people know. The sole talk we hear is of purple heather, as if all heather must be the same. Now, purple is not very common, and this is the only native species of that colour.

The association of purple with heather is a very natural one, and doubtless owes its origin to the fact that this species lends the delightful autumn glow to the hill-slopes, just at the very time when the tourist is on the alert and all the world is in the Highlands. Whereas the delicate rose of the bell heather appeals only to those who are as near as I am now, the mass and glow of the purple is caught from the glen, even by those who are many miles away.

He has enjoyed a rare privilege who has seen

this heather darken under the passing cloud, and blush vividly out again when the shadow has passed over; or the richer, deeper effects as the crimson light of evening comes slant-wise across the purple, as it is doing now. The hue will rest upon the spirit, to fall on the page of the ledger or manuscript, months after, amid the dulness of short winter days and the fog of cities. Little wonder that the dream is of purple heather.

Why it should be called *Erica cinerea*, or grey heath, is not very obvious. In ordinary circumstances its appearance is not grey, but vivid green, supporting one tier or dividing several tiers of bright purple. It retains its glory through many summer and early autumn weeks, and then fades, without, like the rose, becoming ugly.

Widely spread as it is, this is not the commonest heather. A third species is within reach of my hand. Indeed I am reclining on some, half raised above the ground by its wiry springiness. The last to bloom, it is now fully out. The flowers are numerous—small, pink, and pretty. Though there is plenty of it on the far side, I cannot make out the colour at this distance.

It is very vigorous in its growth, and more of a shrub than any of the others; only, it is a lazy shrub. It trails. Were the stems stiff enough to stand upright, it would present the appearance of a dense thicket, through which pathways up the mountain-side would have to be cut. I disentangle one, and pull it out to its full height. Its stature is three feet. Hence its common name — Ling, or Long. Ling is the Highland heather.

Perhaps it is most widely and popularly known as the species amid which visitors wade knee-deep, and totally unconscious of fatigue, for many hours, in their eager search for white heather, con- tented, if, in the evening, they bring back ever so little. It appears as the breezy title to one of William Black's freshest novels. In this way it may be distinguished from the purple in the heatherology of those who before were ignorant of its existence.

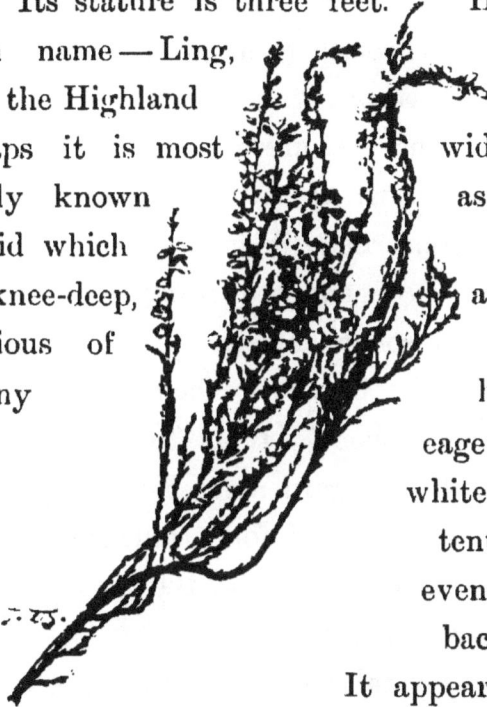

Pinks and kindred colours growing at any considerable height have a tendency to bleach into white. Looking over the face of the hill from where I lie, I can see several distinct shades, some much lighter than the rest. Near the sea the bleaching is still more pronounced. On coast moors I have gathered the fine-leaved heather, with its larger flowers and more decided colour, from purple, through crimson and pink, to purest white. The reasons why ling yields a greater and more certain harvest are probably that it is nearer white, to begin with; and also that, so far as the hills are concerned, it grows, as we shall see directly, in more exposed situations.

It seems a somewhat strange whim that wishes pink heather to be white when there are so many white flowers about. It is the taste, less of a naturalist than a gardener. I understand that a prize has been offered for a blue rose. Were the ling white, there would be the same rush after pink or any other curiosity.

I know several lethargic folk who would not climb a dozen yards for all that nature has to offer, and yet think no labour thrown away in the search for something abnormal. I have seen the precious sprig carefully unwrapped, and displayed as the chief outcome of a month in the Highlands.

The only thing that can be said for the craze is, that it does not hurt anyone else, and probably results in certain indirect benefits. The flush removed from the heather may be confidently looked for in the cheek of the searcher.

These are the only heathers within reach or sight, or for miles around. Indeed there are only three heathers in Scotland; unless I include the trailing azalea on the ridge overhead, and the yew-leaved menziesia confined to the Sow of Atholl. But these, though belonging to the same family, and somewhat resembling them in outside appearance, are not heaths in any strict sense, but mountain plants.

The whole three have been adopted, once and for all, by different Highland clans; from which it appears that these interesting Celts believe them to be distinctive of their elevated regions. I remember an Edinburgh student who wore an eagle's feather in his cap; and it was said that he alone had a right to it, because he was the son of a chief. Since eagles have been bartered by Highland chiefs for grouse, the prejudice ought not to be quite so strong. In some such hostile spirit the favoured tribes may regard any unauthorised

Lowlander or foreigner who affects the rose, the
purple, or the pink.

Towards their summits the highest hills have a
barer look. The heather seems to be thinning out,
as if it were approaching its limit in that direction.
Into this seeming bare region I shall ascend to-
morrow.

From my feet, and also down the opposite slope,
the heather runs away to meet below, or only to
be divided by the breadth of the stream. There
is no appearance of exhaustion, no sign of reaching
any limit that way.

On seaside moor, protected only by the sand-
dunes from the invasion of the waves, I have
found all three round about me, as I do
here. Moorland stretches on the sheltered
inlands, very little above sea-level, yield heather
which seems very vigorous and very much at
home.

However low down I am, there I find myself
with the heather; whereas, if I ascend, I increas-
ingly leave the heather behind. Not all three at
once, but one after the other.

The purple flush does not reach to the top of the
heather region. It ranges only to some fifteen
hundred feet high. By looking keenly, I can just

make out the irregular line where it ceases, or fades into the duller shade above.

The rose heather grows in patches, and nowhere covers a great area. It must be sought after by those who desire it, and may be found in almost any moist place up to about two thousand feet.

That into which the purple fades away is the pink. Hardiest of the three, the ling continues to climb. It alone forms the broad belt of dark shrub, scarcely lit by its blossoms up to the higher alpines. Through it, mainly, one wades for the third thousand feet of the ascent. It is in these higher reaches that the white sprays should be sought for.

This is the Highland heather, in so far as there is such a thing. The crofter puts it to endless uses, and finds it invaluable. To its services as a broom it is said to owe its name, *Calluna*, to cleanse. The more poetic rendering, to adorn, refers to the charm it lends to the surroundings.

The common view, therefore, that Scotland is the natural home of the heaths, because it is so mountainous, is only very partially true. It would be much nearer the truth to say that Scotland marks well-nigh the northernmost limit of the heath zone, and only three of the hardiest of an immense family have been able to penetrate so far.

If hills and hardship had anything to do with it, then the east side of the North Sea is still more favourable. The scene is more broken, the climate severer, and more arctic than our own. If this were a northern type, we should expect to find it flourishing there; whereas the first thing that strikes a visitor to Norway, next to the abundance of alpines, is the scarcity of heaths. This came as a surprise to the experienced members of the Scottish Alpine Club.

"I climbed," says Archibald Geikie, "a slope, clothed with luxuriant masses of ferns, bilberries, and cloudberries;" but no mention of heaths.

We are accustomed to associate grouse and heather. Yet the Norwegian willow grouse, in the absence of that shrub, thrives on something else. Our own grouse are heather birds indeed, alike in tint and diet; but not hill birds, seeing that heather is not a hill shrub. Some were doubtless driven to the slopes, whose sole advantage is their dryness, as a last refuge from the plough. As many still live on the plain as the scanty patches of lowland moor left will support.

The ling alone seems able to bear the severity

of an extreme climate. It penetrates within the polar circle, and appears on the arctic lowlands.

If this is the case toward the north, what about the other direction?

Scarce in Norway, and poorly represented here, the heaths increase in the number of species as they tend farther south. Passing down, in a not very broad belt, they culminate in the south of Africa, where they are known to grow in endless variety and loveliness. Thence all the delightful species which glorify our greenhouses, and may sometimes be coaxed to grow outside, come. The heathers of the Cape, and the primulas of Europe, are the just boast of all who possess them.

Thus, if anyone is justified in using the shrubs as badges, it is not the Highlander, but the South African. I can imagine a Scottish emigrant opening his eyes at the unexpected revelation, and a visitor from the Cape saying, "Do you call that a heath?"

Of the non-Scottish, though British, heathers, there are other three—the spring flowering Irish heath, with racemes of pink flowers, made more attractive by the dark exserted anthers; the large-belled, fringe-leaved heath of Dorset; and the dull, heavy Cornish heath.

These, with their varieties, prefer the milder conditions of the west of Ireland and the south of England; and their affinities are with southern rather than with northern species. Thus the ling of the arctic lowlands, and the vast profusion of the Cape of Good Hope, represent the two extremes.

All this has been said in the interests of exactness, and with no intention of destroying illusions which I most fervently share. There is still enough heather in the Highlands, both for man and grouse.

Long may it be before the search for the white sprig ceases to put the pink of the blossom into the pale cheeks of maidens, and the vision of the purple, even though it actually reveal itself nearer home, lure men "north again."

Long may the holiday seeker—already half recuperated by the prospect—from his corner in "The Flying Scotsman," cry gaily to envious friends on the platform, "For the heather!"

Even if there is not much that is new in her rose or purple or pink, Scotland has still an unapproachable background against which to present them. Never heather on the plain looked like this.

The sun has long dropped out of sight, and the

summits are fast losing their distinctness of outline. The hill-burn is beginning its twilight song, so different, if only in imagination, from that of broad daylight. Shadows are deepening under the woods. The stream runs like a thread of silver down the dimming glen.

Tidy housewives come out to the cottage doors. Their voices reach me here. The saunter down is worse than the climb. I feel wondrous stiff; and tired enough to sleep soundly, even on my procrustean couch.

XIV

ON THE MOUNTAINS

" THIS way to Braemar."

And a finger on the post points away to the right.

"This way to Braemar."

And a second finger, on another post, points to the left.

There is nothing strange in two ways leading to the same place; indeed it is one of the commonest of experiences, the main problem being to find out the shorter one.

One of these ways, so kindly indicated in the freshest of paint and the clearest of letters, has a decided hint of a curve in it.

More suspicious even than that is the quite paternal interest taken in the well - being of pedestrians. There is a difference of opinion here, and two unknown benefactors vie with each other in their zeal to prevent needless wandering. This is unusual in the Highlands, where one is left to grope along as best he can, and is taken roughly to task if, in his ignorance, and to his own great loss of time and strength, he chance to wander.

Now the spirit of these finger-posts is far other than friendly. As soon as one learns why they were put there, the very aspect alters, and they are seen to glare and storm at each other. They represent the very old dispute between private rights and public wrongs. The property has passed out of the hands of one of the old families, and it is the purchaser who kindly recommends the circular route. His finger-post really means, " I wish to shut up the other way."

And the jealous guardians of the sacredness of paths which human feet have trod, time out of mind, without so much as saying, " By your leave," put up their finger-post, which flatly contradicts the other, and says, " You shall not do anything of the kind, if we can help it."

In my experience, the practical victory in all such breezy disputes lies with the proprietor, provided he makes the friction as severe and constant as possible. The timid fear to venture; and even the bold, when they have gone once or twice slowly over the ground, just to show their independence, turn aside from the annoyances, and take the other way.

In this case, the old path happened to be of quite exceptional interest to a small but mildly stubborn order of visitors. Their grievance was not in the closing of the nearest way to Braemar—many of them would have trudged the extra mile or two without a word. The attraction lay along the route, and not in the goal. Lost through all the long hours of a summer day in Glen Doile, they never so much as emerged from the other end. Stained and footsore, but not weary, and with a light shining in their faces, they might have been seen towards night coming out just about where they had gone in. To them the finger-post meant the shutting up of their hilly paradise.

I have no intention of going to Braemar to-day. My further route is in a pleasing state of uncertainty, as it always is when I am abroad. The forbidden ground is just what I have come to see.

There, the gathering majesty of the way passes into still loftier reaches of grandeur and sublimity. Though it gets the name of Doile, it is only the fitting climax where Clova abuts, and abruptly closes, on the tremendous cross - ridge of the

Grampians, forming the backbone of the Highlands.

Nor is it mainly for the scene I have come,—though never for so much as a moment is it possible to lose consciousness of it,—but because these torrent-ploughed slopes form one of the few wild-gardens—certainly one of the first three—of our rarest Scottish alpines.

Like Nelson, I am blind to the signal I do not wish to see, and obey the finger-post which points the nearest way to Braemar as up the glen.

The road passes near the dwelling—I believe it now makes a detour. As I thread my way among the outhouses, I am aware of being the object of a little hostile attention. Loiterers cast a side glance, and disappear into some doorway as if to make my unwelcome presence known. A few moments bring me beyond the shot of eyes into a scene of picturesque wildness—that is, wildness which is not at the same time desolation.

One autumn day—it may be such another as this—a sportsman was shooting over the surrounding heights. His title came from a barren spot in one of the shorter glens opening on Strathmore, watered by the Quharity, dear to all readers of Barrie. His income he owed to a

12

richer property on the banks of the Tay, and a
spirit, which was singularly childlike, to nature
alone.   He paused as his eye fell upon a patch of
rose colour.

It is an excellent thing, when one is alone shooting in these out-of-
the-way places, to
have a pair of eyes
in one's head, and
a soul of some
kind behind
them. The blue
sky, and the
cloud shadows,
and the life and
colour of the
hills, weave tender
threads into the
coarser texture of
a day's sport.
Easily carried about, and a benefit to
the possessor, these simple gifts, as in the case
of this blushing alpine, sometimes notice what
others would like to see and are glad to hear
about.

Few have better opportunities than sportsmen,

if they cared to use them. Compared with their
systematic work, the zig-zagging of an occasional
naturalist is trifling and ineffective, leaving vast
tracks on either hand unexplored. They quarter
every interesting hill in Scotland, cross every yard
of every slope and summit, and that at the bright
season of the year, when all the later and rarer
alpines are in flower. Granting a little natural
curiosity, they might have many a pleasant
revelation to make. Others must have passed
that patch, but no one had thought it worth
his while to pause, or tell over again that such
a thing was there.

But this was a sportsman of the proper sort,
to whom the birds would have been nothing
without the background and the thousand little
touches that made their upland home charming.
In after years he did not think it worth his
while to rehearse how many brace had fallen
to his gun. True, it was before the days of
sensational bags, when, as yet, grouse-shooting
was a gentlemanly sport.

But I have heard him tell, with great anima-
tion, of the delight with which he looked on
that vision of beauty. And I know that it
remained a lovely spot on his memory to the

latest years of his life. The flower had been lost sight of, and the privilege of having found it again made him glad.

With the economy of a lover of nature, who never wastes, however great the wealth may seem to be, he gathered, in remembrance of that Clova idyl. The late Professor Balfour on one of his excursions came that way, and the finder sent a little to where the botanist was staying. It is said that certain playful youngsters of the student band caused the treasure to be placed under cover, and served up for dinner; and we can well believe that the old enthusiast forgot his hunger in his delight.

This wild flower is only reported from the one site, but may have been overlooked on two or three of the heights of the same north-west corner of Forfar. Beyond this restricted area it has only as yet been found in the north of England, where it grows, at a much lower elevation, to a greater height.

This would seem to show it is no denizen of the hills by birth and long tradition, but only one of the Shetland pony order of fairy plants, which, under more favourable conditions, would probably lose its alpine characteristics. I have seen it

flowering freely enough in the gardens of Highland gamekeepers, who had brought a bit away as
they were passing its haunts.

The alpine catchfly, as it is named, presents
a very miniature or fairy semblance of the
extremely pretty crimson day-catchfly, abounding
in most of our moist woods, and brightening so
many of our stream banks; as if the larger flower
had climbed up the hillside, and dwarfed as it
rose higher.

This crimson patch is the goal which, after
visiting the rare corners of the glen, and seeing all
that grows there, I intend reaching.

The day is young, and, for so young a day, is
used up. It has already parted with its morning
freshness—if, in the early hours before I was
abroad, it ever had any. There is sultriness in
the breathless air, and a pitiless glare in the light.
A lit haze fills the glen. Even Clova was open
and breezy in comparison. If it is thus at eleven,
what will it be at two? is a question I am in a
position to answer from my recent experience.
And there is less promise of shelter on these bare
heights. Already it matters not on which side of
a boulder one sits down.

Moreover, the ascent has become sharper, and

the road rougher. There is more of the climb in one's walk. The rush and noise and broken water of the stream alongside is a sufficient measure of the incline.

Eleven is a good time for a rest. It is the hour chosen by outdoor workers, in the sunny months, for placing their backs against the shady side of the stooks. "Eleven hours" they call their fore-noon break. The water is inviting, and here is a bank which will afford the skirt of a shadow.

How brown my hands are! I must be like a mulatto! My last night's lodging had nothing so refined as a mirror, and the water is too broken to see! Stay, there is a quiet place behind the boulder! How still the glen is! The "baa" of the black-faced sheep seems to emphasise the solitude! What is all the fuss about? No one is here to disturb—!

A faint sound, resembling a footstep, reaches me, and, a few minutes afterwards, a man, accompanied by two dogs, appears on the bank overhead. The turn down to the water-side, though not a ruse, has served the same purpose. To all appearance, the man intended following, keeping, as far as possible, out of sight; but, missing me, he had

ventured forward to reconnoitre: there he stands,
revealed in all his brief authority.

Now the positions are reversed. He has to go
on, and I can watch him. It is rather an un-

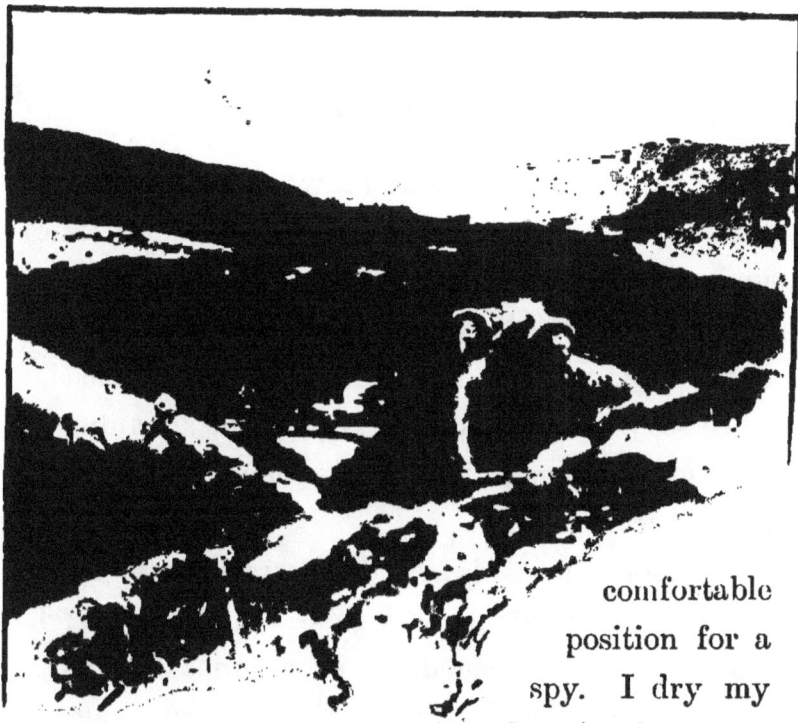

comfortable
position for a
spy. I dry my
feet in the sun—
no very long process—why, they have a tint of
brown on them already; leisurely put on my
boots, and climb up the bank.

My friend is equal to the occasion. In calculat-
ing on any advantage, I have reckoned without
my host. Though he can scarce have got above

two or three hundred yards away, and the glen is
shelterless, save for some tumbled fragments of
rock, he is nowhere in view. Instead of the sullen
up-and-down movements of two tails, and the
flash from a gun barrel, the sun

> All unreflected shone
> On bracken green, and cold grey stone.

He has vanished into thin air, or dropped behind
a boulder, or lain down all his length under some
imperceptible rising of the ground—protectively
coloured in his pepper-and-salt suit. And his
dogs play up to him. Not a hair of them is
to be seen. Once again he regains the advantage;
and so this mountain comedy passes through its
several acts.

An hour afterwards he suddenly reappears—from
nowhere in particular. I look, and he is not; I
look again, and, behold, he is within a few feet.
I seize the chance of asking the nearest way to
the hill on which the catchfly grows. This is
adding insult to injury. He regards me more in
sorrow than in anger, and solemnly warns me
that, so far from helping, he will stand across my
path.

When he sees that the threat has not the desired

effect, he melts into the Highland air, fades into the grass; and, though I never lose the uneasy sense that he is fixing me from behind every stone or tuft of mountain meadow grass, he returns no more.

It is characteristic of these glens in the north-west corner of Forfar, that their wild flowers, with very few exceptions, are much alike. What you find in one, you may look for in the other. And as I shall visit a second, it is the less needful to tell all that grows here.

Indeed, the similarity, if not so close, holds of that concentration of the Highlands, that eternal gathering of the clans, where the three counties of Forfar, Perth, and Aberdeen meet. It may be worth noticing, in the passing, that Perth and Forfar have an equal number of alpines, but not quite the same. Seven are absent from each county, which are present in the other.

The purple mountain milk vetch, so common on seaside links, and again on the lower slopes of hills, passes, at a certain height on Craigmad, into the alpine form, which is mainly white, only tipped with purple. Elsewhere this alpine is found on Craigandree, at Braemar. A similar form, the yellow mountain oxytropis, grows among these hills, and not anywhere else, so far as I know, in Britain.

The sun climbs slowly down as I climb slowly up. On the top I look round for that particular summit, whose shape I partly know. And then I go off in search of the patch of rose, whose charm is certainly not any greater than that of the spirit which once reflected it; which had brought to a halt and gladdened one who was at once a sportsman and a naturalist.

Already are the shadows creeping up the eastern slopes. It will be as easy to reach the next glen as to trudge back to Clova. And the air of my lodging for the night is likely to be fresher.

XV

ON THE MOUNTAINS

IN passing from glen to glen, a break helps one to assimilate experiences which follow so hard upon. A pause between each spell of climbing gives impressions time to print, as well as sort themselves out. Like the scene it represents, a mental picture needs space. If blurred and crowded, it is rather worse than none. Objects must stand a certain distance apart. Haste, so far from being any real gain, finds one at the end of his rambles as well informed as if he had been on a conventional tour over the Continent.

A day or two spent in training the eye to read the mountain-sides from a distance, to tell what wild plant yields that particular hue, to pick out the clump of sphagnum touched with the sundew, to trace the long-leaved cranberry amid the oval-leaved cowberry and blaeberry, is time-saving in

the long-run.   It absolves one ever afterward from
the need of zig-zagging over many a mile in search
of what he wants.   One does not know birds who
can repeat their names when they light on the
fence ; but only he who can tell them at half a
mile away, by their flight and a thousand name-
less traits, marking them off from the rest.

A little pure loitering even, such as a full-length
stretch at midday under the black shadow of the
pine wood, with a run of water and an ample
supply of berries within reach ; or a change of
occupation, such as a twilight cast in the stream,
has its uses in freshening both body and mind.
Jaded energies do not profit much.

Fishing a pool lying in an elbow of the channel,
where the largest trout are known to be, I find
myself breast-high amid the tall purple heads of
the melancholy thistle.   This is perhaps about the
highest reach of the most nearly sub-alpine of the
thistles.

The side-burns I cross at intervals, in passing
down the banks, have their edges touched with the
showy purple of the livelong.   This sedum is
common enough all the way downward to the
plain.   Immediately overhead, it gives place to the
yellow-flowered rose-root, which in its turn reaches

nearly to the summit of the surrounding mountains.

My lodging, so much pleasanter than that of last
night, is in itself a temptation to prolong my stay.
It consists of a room in a cottage overhanging the
stream, where the ripple sings me into dreamland,
and then pleasantly fills up the intervals of sleep.
If the odour of cheese is not altogether absent,
it is not oppressive, and has to be tolerated
in districts so apt to be cut off from supplies,
that the people lay up stores against a long
winter.

The haze of yesterday thickens into vapour,
which passes away in rain. I make the experiment of ascending a mist-covered hill. All knowledge of direction is at once lost. Even the sense
of going up and coming down can no longer be
trusted. But, with a compass, perfect self-
possession, and a close acquaintance with the
sounds and aspects of the scene, one may find his
way. Shepherds and gamekeepers are not
puzzled.

On a delightfully fresh morning, in a rain-
cooled and purified atmosphere, I face toward the
ridge where the glen comes to a dead pause. Isla
is not so mature in its majesty as Clova. It is even

raw and ragged, as if the ploughing glacier had passed over so recently that the lapse of time was too short for mellowing away the effects.

The close, however, is dramatic enough. From the signs of fierce conflict scattered about, there might have been a tussle to force a way through to Aberdeenshire. Wildness has broken loose, and yet the scene is not savage. Picturesqueness is scarcely the word; it is too awe-inspiring for that. One scarce likes to be left alone in its midst, and is all the better of a companion.

The walk is not tiring. No need is there to squeeze into the narrow margin of midday shadow, nor to cool the feet in the somewhat swollen stream.

Wild flowers are even more distinctly sub-alpine than those of Clova. The turf is lit with eye-bright, as gaily as ever Lowland meadow with daisies; while alpine lady's-mantle carpets long stretches of the road.

Through a peat bog I approach the tremendous gateway of the glen, or caen, whose left pillar stands nearly four thousand feet high. I do not enter by the gate, but essay to scale the mighty wall. Turning up the hillside, I ascend into the alpine country. Trailing azalea and other early plants, which make the June hills bright, are past the flowering stage, and, in their sober dress, easily overlooked from a distance.

That pleasant scent is not of whin, but of the bog myrtle on the moister portions of the lower slopes. The shrub of the mountains is not broom, but juniper. As it struggles upward, it dwindles into a bush, which is quite needlessly spoken of as if it were not the same.

In ascending, it is interesting to watch the trees. There are only three to attract attention—the Scots fir, the birch, and the willow. The Scots fir has no alpine representative. It lessens, but is allowed to remain the same species throughout. When it has reached the minimum of size, it is still only a little fir.

The birch cowers closer and closer to the mountain-side or to the rock, until it becomes less a tree than a bush; and each step in the intervening process is represented, so that the eye can follow the passage from one extreme to the other. But the wise conservatism in the case of the Scots fir is departed from; and, as with the juniper, the stunted birch is spoken of as if it were another. The probability is that bush birches are alpines of the Shetland pony kind, which could be passed, in the reverse order, on to the full stature again.

The willow seems to be the only one of the three with truly alpine forms which would probably defy the utmost ingenuity to reconvert into anything else. I see them in increasing numbers as I ascend higher, lying against the face of the slope— little fairy shrubs about the length of a quill-pen, or even less. As one expresses it, root and all might be hidden between the leaves of a lady's pocket-book. Most of them have circular leaves, distinctly and prettily veined and netted. These are not the dwindled forms of the trees at the foot, or the bushes I passed by the way, but differ from both in very many ways.

I begin to notice certain marks, placed evidently by human agency, at stated intervals, and leading in one direction. There are too many of them to be meant for shepherds, who presumably are very much at home on the hills; and they are evidently guides to a more general public.

Glen Isla is a cul-de-sac, much more complete than Clova. The only way out at the top end is to climb. And this route, rising steeply to upwards of three thousand feet, to drop as far on the other side, must be the way to Braemar. The thought calls up the finger-posts of yesterday, with the amusing sequel. Happily, there are not two ways. Nor does there seem scope for any choice up here.

A gamekeeper is on the outlook for me, but this time with no hostile intent. These hills are free to the curious, under the not unreasonable conditions that visitors shall be as careful as possible not to disturb the deer when it is getting near the shooting season. It is a big playground for two to have hide-and-seek in, especially when one is not sufficiently acquainted with the local names to profit by minute directions. With the best intentions in the world, we fail to meet until I call at his cottage in the evening on my way back.

I daresay I missed a little in consequence, for he seemed to be an intelligent man, who had made himself acquainted with all that was interesting in the district. From his knowledge of the hills, he might have guided me more directly to where I wished to go. But there is a good deal in searching out for one's self ; for, even if one does not find out so much, he keeps a better grip of what he has. On this and other visits, I managed to stumble across what was best worth seeing; and I do not think I have forgotten anything.

I had looked on all the forms many times

13

before; and I seek to keep myself as free as possible from that form of curiosity which dearly loves to share a secret, and would fain worm out of every pawky gamekeeper what he has to tell or to sell.

The chief treasure of the place—whose whereabouts, in the opinion of some, all the mountains were placed there to hide—is the snowy gentian. The man who is able to say " I know " is an object of envy. It is a pale blue annual of some three inches high, which peeps over the ledges overlooking the caen in July and August, and rains down its seed alongside and on the ledges beneath, for next year's bloom.

It seems to grow only here and on Ben Lawers. One can account for widely-spread alpines that are found in every likely situation, more easily than for those isolated forms, such as this snowy gentian, or the yellow oxytropis, whose whole area may only extend over a few ledges of rock or a few square yards of turf. How was the seed or pea from which they sprang dropped down ? If their tenure is as ancient as it seems to be, then how, in the many ages before botanists existed, did they not manage to spread farther ?

In contrast with this minute snowy gentian is

the blue sow-thistle. It is a case of the giant and
the dwarf. This sow-thistle—not a thistle—is a
curiosity in its way. The typical alpine is a fairy.
Such is a necessity of its existence. The scanty
food, the exposure, the frequent need to pass
rapidly through the flowering and seeding stages,
all forbid strong or leisurely growth. Minuteness
is the broad distinction between a hill plant and
that of the plain.

The sow-thistle is the only, or at least the chief,
exception. It is an alpine, and yet has the robust
growth of a Lowland form. It grows up the
wildest branch of the gorge. I wish to visit it,
and struggle up under increasing difficulties by
the side of a torrent which rushes ever more rudely
down its boulder-strewn bed. Exhausted, I sit on
a loose rock, upon whose surface, in course of time,
a soil has gathered and shrubs rooted themselves.
Never were such blaeberries, for number and size,
as grow on that rock.

When one turns his face backward after a day's
ups and downs, he begins to feel his sores. There
is now nothing ahead to make him forgetful. His
pace settles down into a certain dogged, uninter-
ested, out-kneed paddling along, which has been
likened to that of the German band.

On looking in upon the gamekeeper, I find him wonderfully good - tempered after his fruitless errand. He shakes his head over the idea of climbing in the mist as foolhardy, and relates some harrowing incidents which had recently occurred on these same hills.

And then he proceeds to describe, in a certain dramatic fashion of his own, the different characters that come there in search of flowers, and the need there is to discriminate. Some of these sketches were worth reproducing, but that there are those who might persist in finding in these pages a looking-glass. From similar reports, and from my own observations, I feel that too much caution can scarcely be exercised if we are to retain the proud distinction of being the land of flowers of a certain very rare and excellent sort.

The risks to our wild plants are not exactly the same, or likely to be so speedily destructive, as those which threaten our wild animals. Any losses up to the present time must be sought for among Lowland forms, through cultivation, drainage, easy access, and other obvious causes.

Probably no upland species has been reduced to the dire straits of some of the birds of prey which dare to find a meal on the moor or in the covert.

They lead a passive and innocent existence, and are in no one's way. Dwelling in a zone of their own, which nothing cares to dispute, they flush the bare slopes with colour, gladden the desolate heights with the signs of life, and furnish a welcome bite to the ptarmigan.

The danger lies rather in the indifference than the hostility of the proprietors, who are careless as to their fate—in many cases ignorant of their very existence. If they keep back the would-be spoiler, it is lest he disturb the game, and not lest he root out the wild flower.

The gamekeeper is more aggressive. His Highland fastness is invaded every summer by eager spirits from the south, such as my friend so graphically described, and he is besieged by questions as to the whereabouts of the alpines. He has taken the hint to look round about him when he is out, and mark the places where anything unfamiliar grows. He uses his advantage skilfully.

He is now ready to supply whatever is wanted for a consideration, and even to guide the more liberal to the spot. Such perquisites make a sensible addition to his wages. Once informed, each newcomer is master of the situation, and may become a guide in turn.

The footsteps of greed desecrate the stillnesses, and the hand of greed lays more waste even than curiosity or false enthusiasm. Where so many are anxious to possess and willing to pay, there are sure to arise sellers; and so quite a trade goes on in alpines. In addition to the amateur who forages for himself and his friends, the professional plant collector is abroad, whose business in life is to hawk on his own account from door to door, or to act on behalf of some man who keeps a nursery.

Two forces are thus at work—the man who lives by it; and a certain uninteresting type of tourists and lodgers, who have not yet learned the first lesson taught to all well-bred children—to look at everything and touch nothing.

It is not so easy to draw the line between a wise conservatism and an unwise interference as many seem to think. There is another side to the access to mountains agitation not visible to those who simply theorise from the plain. Sometimes when abroad on the wilds, with blue cloud-flaked sky overhead, and many-shaded plain three thousand feet beneath, I have been annoyed at the restriction placed on my freedom of movement by some officious gamekeeper.

And before the day was out I have been equally

annoyed at the liberty allowed to another, who was digging and tearing at his own sweet will, and generally doing as much as he could to make the hills not worth climbing.

Something might be accomplished if proprietors once more rose above the commercial spirit, which was wont to be no part of the furnishing of a gentleman, and, setting themselves to find out what was best worth preserving on their respective properties, watched over these with the utmost jealousy—if, among other things, they took as much trouble to make themselves acquainted with their wealth of alpines as some of their servants find it profitable to do.

It might seem Quixotic to suggest a close-time for rare and beautiful plants, to be fixed, as in the case of animals at the breeding-season, when they are flowering and seeding for another generation. But surely the same restrictions which guard our game should be placed around those relics of a glacial age,—which belong to Scotland because she is what she is, which were there before the Celt, or even the earlier race he dispossessed, and are still more a part of the scene than the grouse or the ptarmigan.

XVI

THE SAXIFRAGES

I T is interesting to ask the Lowland wild flowers :
" Have you any kinsfolk among the mountains ?" They will be eager enough to confess,
however roundabout the relationship may be, since
it is esteemed rather an honour, as was his kinship
with the Macgregors in the secret heart of Bailie
Nicol Jarvie.

"My mother, Elspeth MacFarlane, was the wife
of my father, Deacon Nicol Jarvie—peace be wi'
them baith—and Elspeth was the daughter of
Parlane MacFarlane, at the Sheeling o' Loch Sloy.
Now, this Parlane MacFarlane, as his surviving
daughter, Maggie MacFarlane, alias MacNab, wha
married Duncan MacNab o' Stuckavrallachan,
can testify, stood as near to your gudeman,
Robert MacGregor, as in the fourth degree o'
kindred."

Marguerite, Dandelion, and Daisy shake their heads and say they are afraid not.

"Though I am so small and as dainty as they," says the Daisy sadly, "yet I am not an alpine, nor the sister of one."

Perhaps the Marguerite is least concerned, as being a soft eyed and rather stately Lowland maiden, who has no wish to be stunted.

The Primrose answers, rather vaguely, that she has heard of a relative, not in the hills indeed, but beyond them, who dresses ever so prettily in lilac, not in common yellow. Her cousin, the cowslip, once met her in Caithness.

"Lots," says the Lady's-mantle. "Next time you go to the Highlands, just mention my name, and they will come trooping down to the glen-mouth to meet you."

"Not so common as that," says that blushing coquette, the Day-catchfly. "There is just one little clan of my family that lives apart and quite select on their native hill. Some have been here on a visit, and seemed to like the place very well, although they kept to the grand garden, and never came out to see me here by the water-side."

"We believe we have," says the blue-eyed Forget-me-not — who could forget her? — and

Veronica, "but they are far too high for such as we."

One would like a word with the gentians, if one only knew where to find them. They are absent from the hedgerow. They do not enter the woods, or lodge by the burn-side. There is not one, so far as I know, within miles of where I am at the present moment. So that most people have never seen any of them, and only a few know them, even by name.

The most accommodating of all still likes a matured piece of turf, or a firm springy river-bank, such as is not to be found everywhere. One appears here and there among the bents along the coast.

The handsomest of a charming family is one of the few British alpines absent from Scotland— alpine only as the crimson catchfly is—since it courts the soft Atlantic winds on the mild west coast of Ireland, and sets up its blue tent for a few spring weeks on the lower heights of Teesdale. The snow form holds the ledges of one of our four mountain gardens.

I have met these gentians in many situations, and never a tame one—in Shetland, in Orkney, amid unbented sand-dunes and bare precipices.

And to me they partake of the wildness, oft weird-
ness, of their haunts.

Say to the Saxifrage, "Have you any Highland
kin ?"

"It would be more to the purpose to ask if we
have any Lowland ones," will be the stiff reply.
"Or, should we be so unfortunate, will a stream
of rushing water acknowledge any relation
with the portion withdrawn from it for the
mean domestic uses of those who dwell on the
banks ?"

So like their Highland pride! And yet the boast
would be true. They are our hill plants *par
excellence.* Nor is it enough to call them the
alpine of our alpines. They are that, and something more. They overflow the hills into more
distant and drearier regions.

Just about the time when the blue violets are
at their best, there appears among them a showy-
white flower, not recumbent as they are, but upright, and twice as tall. It does not cover all the
area of the violets—never, so far as I know, stray-
ing into the woods. It selects where the turf is
fairly firm and old, with a marked preference for a
slope. Such is the only Lowland relation of the
saxifrages ; but for which they could claim, as far

at least as Scotland is concerned, to be a purely Highland clan.

This meadow haunter never ventures north so as to enter the home of the Macgregors, the stronghold of the saxifrages. Did it seek to scale the "promontory by one or two rapid zigzags along the precipitous face of a slaty-grey rock, which would otherwise have been inaccessible," it would only be to find these rude places held by relatives indeed, but such as might give it scant welcome. The feud between Celt and Saxon has been healed, but not that between Highland and Lowland plants.

Much about the same time that the white is adding to the brightness of the plain, the opposite leaved saxifrage is lending an early flush of purple to the hills. This is the form so very popular in our gardens as a rockery plant. It grows wild in these early months, when few are there to see.

One must wait a month or two after the spring meadow form has faded, and the autumn holiday enables him to leave the plains for the hills, before he will see any more saxifrages.

The first to greet him as he breasts the slopes, just after the earliest flush of heather has crept over them, is the yellow mountain saxifrage—not a form requiring to be searched for; it runs along the fenceless paths which wind round the mountains, between the bracken and the heather, with all the freedom and at-homeness of one of our commonest plants. A hillman would no more think of turning to look at it, than we at so many daisies and buttercups.

And yet, if it be the first time in those parts, one needs to waken up, so strangely unlike are they to anything he is accustomed to. Even now, often as I have been with them, I find myself pausing in wonder. There is that about alpines which makes them wild flowers indeed, and not simply by courtesy. They are rare, in the most delicate sense of that word.

Such experiences as these bring out the differences between mountain and lowland. The Highlands are a new world of fresh forms, and owe their attractive as well as recuperating influence to the fact. On the Glen Isla hills this yellow may be gathered by the cart load.

The range of the white starry saxifrage comes not quite so far down, though it is found on the lower slopes of the hills. In many places it seems to be the more abundant of the two. One who has not seen it growing—say, in some rift of the rock exposed by the wearing of the mountain torrent—cannot even imagine how lovely it is, or how fitly it is named. White, and starry, and saxifrage—how charming must that, which has three such names, be !

Indeed, both these forms are lovely—at once the fairest and the commonest of the tribe. If it were not for fear of consequences, I should say to all Lowlanders, " See them this very autumn, and learn what natural loveliness, when in its proper environment, is." Learn, too, how altogether the saxifrage is a child of the mist and of the rocks— not a stone breaker, but a stone adorner, in which the spirit of the scene looks out.

From these, which thus cluster round the dividing line between hill and plain, I pass at a stride over many interesting forms to the rarest of all— those that are in the act of disappearing from the mountain-top into space.

If one climbs Lochnagar and searches diligently enough, he may find the snowy and the brook saxifrages. And if one knows where to look on Ben Lawers, he will see the one site in Scotland where grows the drooping saxifrage.

These two, Ben Lawers and Lochnagar, are the Aberdeen and Perthshire wild-gardens respectively, just as Caenlochan and Glen Doile are those of Forfar. The four form the alpine haunts of Scotland. Other mountains and gorges have forms, it may be, even peculiar to themselves, but in none are so many gathered into one place.

All who have seen the cotyledon growing in gardens must have rejoiced in it, wondered if anything so perfect could be wild, and, if so, what land was favoured with its presence. Yet it grows in Norway, amid other saxifrages — not sparingly, but so freely as to form a marked feature of many scenes. Those who have seen it in the open, with its great top-heavy trusses, speak of it with the utmost enthusiasm.

From Norway the saxifrages tend farther northward till they enter within the arctic circle.

There are really three divisions among our alpines, with no very distinct lines between, but still rudely separable. Some are simply stunted Lowland plants, whose tendency is distinctly southward. These I have spoken of as Shetland pony alpines.

Others are in their proper places on the hills, where they lead the little intense life peculiar to the fairy kind, in pure enjoyment. They exult in their lofty dwelling-place; their favourite food is

the schist, their breath the hill breezes. They
tend neither northward nor southward. These
are the true alpines.

There are those which are at once alpines and
arctics. They appear at a certain high altitude,
from which they climb up to the loftiest summits;
and beyond that, they are found at sea-level in
the polar regions, where they grow with the
freedom of natives. To this division belong the
saxifrages.

Several of our hill, and even of our heath plants,
chiefly among the shrubs, go north. Even a few
denizens of the plain are given to eccentric movements. The poppy—that vagrant of our waste
places and cornfields—passes over our hills without
stopping (possibly because they are too windy to
light on), and beautifies the arctic lowlands. The
summer there, if short, is thus made gay while it
lasts.

To those who associate only desolation with the
far north, the following picture from the dreary
east coast of Greenland, by the hand of Nansen,
may come as a surprise.

"A little past noon we reached a small island,
which seemed to us the loveliest spot we had ever
seen on the face of the earth." And we must

remember that Nansen was familiar with the rich alpine flora of Norway. "There was grass, heather" (which must have been the ling), "sorrel, and numbers of bright flowers. It was a simple paradise, and wonderfully delightful we found it, to be stretched on the green sward, in the full blaze of the sun. There we gathered a few flowers, in memory of the little Greenland idyl."

The bright flowers would doubtless include many poppies—it may be, in marshy places, a few buttercups; but by far the greater number would be the various saxifrages.

The saxifrage is the arctic flower. As soon as the snows rise, it appears. Wherever black earth or black rock is exposed, it takes possession. It is the first and most daring of explorers. No place so northernly that it may not visit. It seems to be able to cross barriers of white that never melt. In one of the recent Arctic Expeditions the saxifrage was seen to cling to a piece of rock protruding from the snow—

> It comes before the snowbird dares, and takes
> The northern wind with beauty.

Everyone knows that once upon a time the ice-field lay very much farther down over the Continent, banishing every living thing to the

South of Europe. Our own land was practically wiped out, buried fathoms deep. As the sheet slowly shrank and retreated northwards, life followed and took possession.

Among plants, the hardier and smaller were in advance; the larger and more succulent waited till the chilled and sodden earth was warmed and dried, and the danger of devastating floods was past. The English Channel was then a land valley, so that no obstacle checked the onward march.

For a while the first comers had all this land to themselves. They were satisfied with little, could endure much, and were able to cling to any support. above the reach of the tumbling waters, caused by the melting of the ice. They held possession of the lowlands, the hills being capped with white, and the glens blocked with glaciers.

As the climate became still milder, and the ice-field shrank farther back, the main body of big strong plants ventured forward. Unable to contend with those luxuriant growers on their · own ground, the snow flowers took to the hill-slopes. Closely followed, they clambered yet higher up, seizing on every nook and coign of vantage, rooting themselves wherever they could find a sprinkling of soil or a crack in the rock. Thus snow plants were changed into alpines.

At length they reached an altitude where they could defy competition. There they have remained from that distant time till now, and there they will remain so long as they are fairly dealt by. Districts where the land was mainly flat, or the heights were only moderate, —less, say, than two thousand feet,—gave no refuge to the first comers against their pursuers. Those that ventured to climb were caught as in a trap, and killed out. Such places number no alpines in their flora.

But Forfar, Aberdeen, and Perth, chiefly near where the three counties meet, offered the heights of Monega, Mad Crag, Lochnagar, and, a little farther off, Ben Lawers, together with such stern defiles as Caenlochan, Caenness, and Glen Doile. Therefore it comes to pass that we are so rich in hill plants.

Certain of the fugitives planted garrisons or contingents on the hills by the way, while the main body followed on the track of the ice, after it had left our land bare from Tweed to Shetland. Chief among such were the saxifrages, which thus became at once hill plants and snow plants, alpines and arctics.

And so the division arose between our arctic alpines, which followed on—our alpines, which made themselves at home on the hills, and sent no representatives north, and our plain plants, which were not robust enough either to climb or to follow.

XVII

AMONG THE SOUTHERN UPLANDS

TO pass from the Highlands to the Borders
is of the nature of an anti-climax. Nothing
here was lofty enough to give shelter to such
snow plants as may have retreated up their sides.
The southern uplands are moorland and sub-
alpine.

What rare wild flowers there are, may best be
shaded off by what are missing. No rare
saxifrages, no snowy gentian, no rock speedwell,
no mountain forget-me-not, of the northern alpine

area, grows on those more moderate heights with their shallower glens.

I am settled by the Border stream, and looking forward to a long walk over the hills. This is in the yearly round. It has been my delight to make myself as much at home on the heights above the Tweed as on those of the Perthshire Tay and the Forfar Isla and Esks.

Several days are spent in getting myself into condition. In my day and night fishing I have done a good deal of tumbling up and down the banks; but climbing is a thing apart, and needs a training by itself.

I start up one of the wild side-glens of this portion of the valley. The burn, innocent-looking as it is to-day, responds like an untamed colt to the lightest lash of a cloud, by breaking into a gallop, or clean taking the bit between its teeth and careering headlong down.

Oppressively desolate and lonely at first, these glens take possession of one after a while, and become wonderfully attractive. A day with the rod is pleasant, if only as a strong contrast to casting along the milder course of the Tweed. One gets used to the crossing and recrossing of the sheep over the stony channel. So, too, do the trout. The paddling of the "trotters" does not seem to scare or keep them from taking the hook.

Countless little springs, without the strength to form a channel or a current to lend them character, sipe through the grass on to the road, to find some hidden way into the stream. Their moist track down the slope is marked by the purple of hairy sedum, by the pink of alpine willow herb, and the yellow of the marsh buttercup.

The goal is Windlestrae Law—the highest hill in the neighbourhood. The peak—more than two thousand feet above—is, as yet, hidden from sight by intervening ridges. A slope, not very steep in itself, is so beset with shrubs as to put one's endurance to the test. There is no escaping a wide belt of heather. Ling, in this case, certainly deserves its name, being longer than usual.

Heather, when knee-deep, so that one cannot very conveniently lift each step clear over the top, is very troublesome to walk among. From its recumbent habit, it has a nasty tendency to catch one just above the boot.

Three feet of ling, two of which are trailing, is not only a drag, but very much of a trap as well.

In case of undue haste, one is apt to be tripped up and rolled over and over among the pink blossom. The latter experience mainly overtakes one in running down - hill. Climbing is too serious a business in itself for any such frivolity.

The moist places are thickly dotted with sphagnum, both stout and fragile; and of all pleasant shades, from very pale to ruby-tipped. The fleecy water variety floats out on the little dark pools of the peat. Much of it—more, I think, than ever I saw before—is in fruit. In my mental register, that experience is noted down as "A day among the sphagnums." In my little map, which no one ever sees, Windlestrae is named Sphagnum Hill.

A day among the cloudberries, too. These smallest of our native brambles seem well-nigh to cover the summit. Many bear fruit. Some are in flower—a very pretty white blossom, like the rest of the brambles. One entire cloudberry, root and all, I put into my buttonhole, and wear for the rest of the day.

The boggy ground—rather too boggy, in some places, for comfort—seems to suit the plant. It is pretty widely distributed under similar conditions, and is perhaps more characteristic of these uplands than any other form. It is as near an approach to

an alpine as we are likely to find.   Since there can
be no rivalry between a moss and a wild flower,
Windlestrae also appears on my map as " Cloudberry Hill."

A very early hour of the second morning after
finds me dropping behind a curtaining ridge, out
of sight of the placid Tweed.   Before me, a
pastoral region slopes down to form the banks of
the stream, and melts away over the gently
rounded hilltops.

The vale is suggestive of undefined emotions
and pensive thoughts.   Appealing to the imagin-
ative and impressionable of bygone days, it has
found utterance in sad and tragic ballads.   Who
says that a scene may not have a character?   Is
it fancy that there are lines of ineffaceable sorrow?
I sit down by Yarrow-side to rest.   The way left
behind, though not long,—only ten miles,—needed
a good deal of stiff climbing.

The whole morning had been delightful.   As yet
there is no hint of change to quicken the pace
—only a little mist on the distant hills ahead,
whence the gentle airs come.   A leisurely saunter
along the even ground will be a pleasant contrast
to the ups and downs.

The lake is a part, the eye of the scene. As in the

case of other eyes, much of the expression is there
—reflection among the rest. Its shadows are reflec-
tions, in the deeper sense. Sad St. Mary's! A good
deal is in that "sad." In its silent depths, memories
lie. When I come in sight, it is in one of its
quieter moods, not cheerful; it never is—only still.

Even as I look, the aspect changes: the trouble
comes to the surface, the face darkens, the spirit
of gloom sweeps over it with a moan. Out of the
dark cloud comes the rain. Storm on St. Mary's
has something of a human outburst in it. Rain
falls with the bitter significance of tears.

Five minutes are long enough to wet one
through. The seven miles to "Tibbie's" become a
dogged walk with water—water everywhere, from
cap and finger-tips to boots. The Selkirk coach
has just come in, full of passengers. There is no
getting near the fire, and the floor looks miserable
with the drippings.

A lull tempts me out again. Along the shores
of "the Lake of Lowes" the mist-winged storm
comes along worse than ever. Now all is natural.
The sadness has dropped behind—only, the wildness is in the mountain fastness, from which the
wind and the mist come forth, to play roughly on
the plain.

The ascending road leads into the midst of the fray—into the very presence of the raider. The storm takes visible form in the mist which sweeps past—swirls, lifts for a moment to reveal a few yards of the hillside, and then, for a like brief interval, settles round, wrapping me to my very clothes.

Two hours later, when I am beginning to think that I have been the plaything of the elements about long enough, I come suddenly on shelter. I do not see the cottage until I can almost touch it. In some of the stiller moments of the storm I must have passed unawares; but the veil lifts, and there it is.

The thought of lodging had not troubled me when I started, nor in the earlier hours of the day. If it came, good and well; if not, then the earth was big enough. But I had not reckoned on this. Certain who preceded me, tell of their experience in the same neighbourhood :— ,

"As there were large quantities of the common bracken, we unanimously resolved to bivouac there for the night; and having partaken of our evening meal, and drunk from the clear gushing stream, we laid ourselves down to sleep, with the sky above as our curtain, and the majestic hill at our backs and on either side as our bed-posts. Our love for the romantic seemed now to be indulged to the full; and what strange thoughts came into our heads as we peeped out through the ferns which grew so thickly around us!

"One by one we dropped to sleep; but scarce had we shut our eyes, when our hands, which we had left outside the covering as barometers, told us of a change of weather. We should soon have been drenched had we not taken up our beds and adjourned to a hut, which, to all appearance, served as a maternity hospital for all the sheep in the neighbourhood.

"It was now twelve o'clock, with the rain pouring in torrents, and the wind whistling in fitful gusts through our fragile domicile, and one of our sorrowing friends was heard to whisper—

> Sic a night
> As ne'er puir sinner was abroad in."

Sic another night was this, and such mayhap would have been my fate had the storm delayed its coming. In my weakness, the prospect of a tighter roof brings a sense of relief. I had been here before.

A shepherd's cottage has been converted into a sort of hostelry, for the behoof of passers through the defile. In old days it might have been called

a "Spital." The house is full; there is not much
to fill. I might not have been lodged at all, but
that it was a night

> Wherein the cub-drawn bear would couch,
> The lion and the belly-pinched wolf
> Keep their fur dry.

Even the four dogs are inside.

The shepherd's wife not only takes me in, but
clothes me. The suit is her husband's. I never
saw the wearer, who was away at Peebles Fair
with the season's lambs; but I have good reason to
suppose that he is twice my weight.

For two whole days I live and move and have
my being in these clothes. I revel in them, tent
in them, roll about in them, insist that my own are
not dry, until the kindly lender laughingly asks if
I would like to take them away with me.

Anglers gather in from the streams, or are blown
in by the gusts which set every door a-rattling and
every inmate a-shivering. No one has been successful. Rising water seldom yields a basket. Trout
are too much concerned in looking after themselves,
and in seeking the eddies which are last to be
blotted out.

These men have been tempted up from Moffat by
the rain-bearing clouds, which blew from that direc-

tion, and had got more than they wanted. The
coach rattles up and takes them off. The house is
left to those who are to stay there.

"I would just hae to be doin' wi' a seat at the
kitchen fire, as the room was let to a lady and
gentleman frae Liverpool."

That is how my hostess puts it. Worse fate by
far might have befallen me.

Happily, the gentleman overhears, and courteously invites me to join them. The blind is
drawn, the lamp lit, and chairs placed round the
table. In a rubber of whist we forget the storm,
or only hear it at intervals, to the increase of our
sense of comfort by contrast. The louder it raves,
the more we hug ourselves. Had you ever a
rubber of whist under similar conditions? If so,
you will know all it means.

I am abroad, bright and early. Never fresher
morning broke over these or any other hills. The
son, a shepherd like his father, is called in, and
gives minute directions how to go so as to avoid
the peat-hags. I am sure I understand him, and
so take my way up the slope. The sundew grows
in moist places; so does the water forget-me-not,
the rarest of its kind to be found on these hills.

Of course I do not avoid the peat-hags. Indeed

I get into the very midst of them; and having once lost a track, at best so faintly indicated that only a shepherd could follow, I never recover it. More than once I have to descend my own height on to a treacherous-looking black bottom, rendered none the firmer by yesterday's rain. By sheer persistence I somehow bore my way to Loch Skene.

The mountain sorrel is everywhere. The small crowded flowers, rising above the kidney-shaped leaves, are effective, from the reddish tint they share with the rest of the family. Natural beauty owes much to lowly agents. The wilds could better spare many a brighter flower. This is a sub-alpine that passes into the lower alpine regions, and after that reappears, to give a welcome touch of colour to the arctic lowlands. It is thus interesting, as being one of the northernly tending arctic alpines.

The mossy saxifrage, so familiar in our gardens for its cushions of much-cut leaves, is the commonest of the few — three, I think — sub-alpine species growing on these hills. The other two are the starry and opposite-leaved saxifrages.

Still another plant — the alpine enchanter's nightshade—is characteristic. The ordinary species covers the floor of some of the woods lower down. Neither is to be regarded as strictly lowland; and the alpine form may only be the other, modified by changed conditions. Both have in their fantastic flowers a certain weird suggestiveness of their name, especially when growing in the shade.

Somewhere around, a friend, who had his home by the Tweed-side, once made an experiment. He was a rare man, such as one meets among the common herd only twice or thrice in a lifetime. Dearly he loved these alpine fairy plants; and he had a strong wish to get others to care for them as well, and to take a pleasure in climbing the hills to look at them.

Out of very unpromising elements he formed an Alpine Club, which exists to this day, although its pure and noble guide is gone. There are those who reserve such words as unpractical for such schemes as these; but this one, happily, for those who became a part of it, took shape. Some who ran the ordinary risks of becoming sordid, feel all the better for a day on the hills which overlook their homes and dwarf their everyday lives.

My friend, naturally, wished to see his favourites as often as possible. But it was a long way to

come ; and, living so far apart as they did, he could
visit only two or three at a time. He was, for all
the world, like a man whose children are scattered,
and who grieves that he can no longer have them
all together as he used to do. So he fixed upon a
common home, and spent a few summer days in
tenderly gathering two or three of each, and
placing them as near together as their differing
habits would allow.

One can picture the scene. I think, by patient
search, could pick it out. And it would be
worth finding; for if ever spot on earth was
hallowed by the purity and simplicity of man, that
spot was.

It would be bordered by a channel, whose rocky
shelving, laid bare by the rude torrent, gave root-
hold to the starry saxifrage. It would include a
marshy area, tender with the blue of forget-me-not,
white with mountain avens, and touched with the
red of sundew. It would possess a shadow,
quaintly pretty with the spikes of enchanter's
nightshade; and a rough track lit with the scarlet
fruit of the stone bramble, and overrun with the
white purple - tipped blossoms of the wood vetch.
These at least.

Alas ! for the best laid schemes. His face wore

15

a half-vexed, half-amused look as he told me the
sequel.   One day he reached his paradise, to find it
despoiled ; and, some time afterward, he learned the
cause.   Certain botanists from Edinburgh, with
vascula of greedy dimensions, came by chance that
way, and doubtless reported the spot as an extremely rich floral area.

Loch Skene is flanked on one side by Whitcoom,
which shows its summit just over the sub-alpine
region — some two thousand six hundred feet
above sea-level.   This mountain is interesting as
forming the culminating height in these parts ;
moreover, it stands at the touching point of Selkirk,
Peebles, and Dumfries.

In these uplands, Whitcoom holds a position
similar to that of those other culminating heights
which at once attach and separate Aberdeen, Perth,
and Forfar.   It is the hilly centre and stronghold
in the south, as they are in the north.

What is not found here need scarcely be looked
for elsewhere.   And yet the chief rarities its
slopes have to offer are the alpine meadow rue, the
cranberry, and the veined willow.

If they fell within the popular notion of wild
flowers, it would delight me to talk about the ferns ;
the rather as I regard these hills as the fern

garden of Scotland, just as I regard the northern hills as the alpine garden. If some of the rarer forms are absent, those which are there, abound.

The brittle fern, the most graceful of all the forms—and what is rarity, compared with grace, except to the dry-as-dust naturalist — is, in many places, as common as the bracken or the grass.

The male parsley fern waves above the wastes of stones, and hides away the rudeness under its feathery fronds: the oblong Woodsia is common here—a corrie or linn, in the flank of this same Whitcoom, is a favourite haunt; while the filmy fern, in countless numbers, seems to filter every drip of water.

Before leaving the hostelry, I open the visitors' book and run down row upon row of uninteresting names. On turning over a page, my eye is arrested by the sketch of a tourist's back, with fishing-basket and other belongings of sport and travel strapped thereon as if for final departure. The man who did this knew the use of his pencil.

The lines beneath, which I quote, less because of their literary merit—the author was not so much

at home with the pen—than for the pathos and
human interest behind a rude form, ran thus—

Scottish lakes are bonnie,
Scottish hills are high,
So are Scots hotel bills—
Scotland, good-bye !

PRINTED BY
MORRISON AND GIBB LIMITED, EDINBURGH

www.ingramcontent.com/pod-product-compliance
Lightning Source LLC
Chambersburg PA
CBHW030322270326
41926CB00010B/1462